All the Presidents' Memories

How they Reconstruct the Past,
Manage the Present and
Shape the Future

~

Volume II

By Henry J. Roth, Ph. D.

Cover and interior design by Lorraine Sharon Roth.
   —Statue of William Henry Harrison located in Cincinnati, Ohio, with plaque, "Ohio's First President."
   —"Horse boy with rocking horse" grey vintage photograph card, Donna Arishenkoff Jenkinson. brbl-images.library.yale.edu

Roth, Henry J. (Joseph) 1949-
All the Presidents' Memories/ Henry J. Roth, Ph.D.

ISBN-13: 978-1976263446
ISBN-10: 1976263441

1.   Non-fiction; 2. History; 3. Presidents of the United States; 4.
     Compelling Personal Memories; 5. Early Memories

10 9 8 7 6 5 4 3 2 1

Also by Henry J. Roth, Ph.D.:

Climbing Jacob's Ladder: Teaching and Counseling Orthodox Students © 2003

Tales from Time-Out © 2008

Techniques for Time-Out: A Study Guide and Workbook of Behavior Management and Counseling Strategies © 2013

All the Presidents' Memories: How they Reconstruct the Past, Manage the Present, and Shape the Future ~ Volume I © 2016

"While I wear [an officer's] sword & the livery of my country I will not disgrace them by owning myself inferior to any person."

~ William Henry Harrison

"If it becomes necessary I'll take command of the army myself and if you are taken in rebellion against the Union I will hang you with less reluctance than I hanged deserters and spies in Mexico."

~Zachary Taylor

"It is a relief to feel that no heart but my own can know the personal regret and bitters sorrow over which I have been born to a position so suitable for others rather than desirable for myself."

~Franklin Pierce

"When I sum up the many taunts, the gotton-up, and intended slides to me and mine, all without cause so far is known, I wish from the bottom of my heart that we were all blotted out of existence, and even the remembrance of things that were."

~Andrew Johnson

" I so much despise a man who blows his own horn that I go to the extreme of not demanding what is justly my do."

~James Garfield

"I have imagined that at some future time I could do considerable, but the more I learn, the more I feel my littleness

~Rutherford B. Hayes

"If I had misappropriated five cents, and on walking downtown saw two men talking on the street together, I would imagine they were talking of my dishonesty, and the very thought would drive me mad."

~Chester A. Arthur

"I want it understood that I am the grandson of nobody. I believe that every man should stand on his own merits."

~Benjamin Harrison

Acknowledgment

Collaborating on this book with my wife, Lorraine, provided an enduring memory of our affection and love for each other. It is comforting to be reminded of how encouraging she has been in all aspects of writing this book, including her creativity in designing the cover. Her keen insight, depth and ability to motivate and inspire me is a memory worth keeping forever.

TABLE of CONTENTS

INTRODUCTION

Lincoln once said, "I am slow to learn and slow to forget that which I have learned." This book describes what eight Presidents "slowly" learned from their early memories, and how they were "slow to forget" the lessons of those memories as they grew older.

- A memory of his home being ransacked by Benedict Arnold created a unique historical identity for William Henry Harrison and helped to define his revolutionary image. It is not difficult to see how Harrison's military actions at the Battle of Fallen Timbers was influenced by his earliest memory.

- A memory revealing the hardships that faced people living on the frontier helped to shape Zachary Taylor's expectations in dangerous situations, and his willingness to initiate the necessary adjustments in the Battle of Okeechobee. As a result, he was given the name "Old Rough and Ready."

- A memory of his father who was a Brigadier General in the Revolutionary War depicted the origin of Franklin Pierce's patriotism and his desire to become a soldier and command troops in battle.

- A memory about his early life in poverty functioned as a catalyst for Andrew Johnson to initiate bold actions to overcome it. One can see how the wish to gain respect from those who had looked down on him in the memory led to his brashness as the Military Governor of Tennessee with the rank of Brigadier General.

- A memory rooted in themes of familial harmony, conflict and reconciliation, helped to shape the identity of Rutherford B. Hayes. The memory offered a preview of how he would later earn the admiration of his soldiers by treating them as if they were extended members of his own family.

- A memory describing the difficult and dangerous circumstances that James Garfield faced as he stood on the bow of a boat provided him with the motivation to rise to the top. This same determination that he showed in the memory distinguished him at the Battle Chickamauga.

- A memory that showcased Chester A. Arthur as a resourceful and capable leader provided him with a sense of confidence that helped him to become an effective leader in his capacity as Quartermaster General during the Civil War.

- A memory of the power of prayer called attention to something inside of Benjamin Harrison that was longing for inner peace, solitary reflection and spiritual guidance. As a General, Harrison applied the lessons of the memory in promoting a religious and prayerful atmosphere in the camps.

Just as each President cited in this book had military experiences that helped to ready him for the presidency, each also had his earliest memories to ready himself for the future. How their beliefs, attitudes, military principles and political convictions emerged from their earliest memories becomes the focus of this book.

The eight Presidents in this volume are added to the four in Volume I who also served as Generals in the military: George Washington, Andrew Jackson, Ulysses S. Grant and Dwight D. Eisenhower.

William Henry Harrison
President of the United States
March - April 1841

As a child who grew up during the American Revolution, William Henry Harrison's early memories depict several events that helped to shape his character:

Memory One: "A Child of the Revolution"

William Henry Harrison was born February 9, 1773. At the age of nine, he witnessed Hessian troops and American loyalists, under the leadership of Brigadier General Benedict Arnold, march through and sack the Harrison family plantation at Berkeley, Virginia. The Harrisons learned in advance that the soldiers were on a mission to seize Richmond, and were able to flee to safety to avoid being personally attacked. Nevertheless, the furnishings, family paintings and other treasures in the Harrison home were destroyed, livestock were slaughtered, and slaves and horses were captured. The ravaging of the house was so devastating that the family did not move back until three years later.

—*William Henry Harrison,* by Henry Green, Page 1.

The memory highlighted young Harrison's first-hand experience of the Revolutionary War, inspiring the fervent patriotism that would become a central focus in his life, and setting the stage to cast himself as a "child of the revolution" during the 1840 presidential campaign. The implication was that Harrison personified the values and traditions of America's past and was the right person to restore the country to the revolutionary ideals on which it was founded: establishing a strong and united country, respecting the dignity of the common man, promoting self-determination, and remaining vigilant against the concentration of power. The memory was more than just an account of a traumatic experience—it provided Harrison with a moral imperative to honor and revere his revolutionary roots. William's father, Colonel Benjamin Harrison, was among the most important leaders in Virginia and one of the delegates to the First Continental Congress, as well as the second person to sign the

Declaration of Independence. William's father was an intimate friend of George Washington and roomed with him during the Continental Congress. Colonel Harrison was a member of the Virginia House of Delegates and served three terms as Governor of Virginia. His mother, Elizabeth Bassett Harrison, came from one of Virginia's earliest and most prestigious families and was a relative of Martha Washington. According to biographer Henry Green, as a youngster, William Henry Harrison recalled witnessing other Revolutionary-related events such as French and American troops moving to surround the British; hearing gunfire from Yorktown; and dining with George Washington as well as other luminaries who were visiting Berkeley.

William could take comfort and pride in a memory in which he viewed himself as a credible historic link between the Revolutionary forefathers and the best interests of the United States. In the painful aftermath of the destruction of the Harrison estate, the memory provided William with proof that he could survive a series of devastating events and grow stronger as a result. Overcoming adversity may have also suggested to William that there was a silver lining behind the cloud of loss and destruction—even if British forces had removed and destroyed everything in the Harrison home, a new and vibrant nation was created. The British had not taken away young William's indomitable spirit or his capacity to imagine himself as a General or President—someone who could lead the charge against abusive authority.

Viewing himself as a survivor through the lens of the memory, William tried to prove the point to the nation during the 1840 Presidential campaign. In portraying himself as a "child of the revolution," the memory may have been saying, "See, here's the proof: my family suffered loss, destruction and devastation in the Revolutionary War. As your President, I will be uniquely qualified to resolve inequities in our political and economic system."

In the memory, Harrison's enduring concern for what happened to his family found extension in his compassion for the poor. Harrison identified the power of the rich as the fundamental difference between the nation's revolutionary roots and the period of the

1840's in which he was elected President. During the 1840 campaign he said, "All the measures of the government are directed to the purpose of making the rich richer and the poor poorer." In his Inaugural address, Harrison claimed that monied interests used their insidious influence to undermine equality and social justice. Harrison also admonished America to be aware of the negative influence of government subsidies: "We have learned, too, from our own as well as the experience of other countries, that golden shackles, by whomsoever or by whatever pretense imposed, are as fatal to [liberty] as the iron bonds of despotism."

The memory memorialized the suffering of the Harrison family and the wreckage of their estate. At the same time, it may have represented the origin of Harrison's belief in a more humane and just society. For example, even though the Harrison family owned slaves, William wrote the following, "At the age of 18, I became a member of an Abolition Society established at Richmond, Virginia; the object of which was to ameliorate the condition of slaves and procure their freedom by every legal means."

William was tutored at home and at age 11 enrolled at Hampden-Sydney Academy where he studied the classics. Trustees on the college board included figures such as Patrick Henry and James Madison. His father viewed Hampden-Sydney Academy as too influenced by loyalists and Methodists, so his father pulled him out of the school at age 14. His father wanted him to be a doctor so William began the study of medicine in Richmond in 1791, at age 18. Subsequently, he went to Philadelphia to pursue his medical studies with the father of American psychiatry, Benjamin Rush.

 At 18, William's father died; and rather than following his father's wish for him to pursue the field of medicine, he decided to follow his own dream to begin a career in the military. William was encouraged in making this decision by Henry "Light-Horse Harry" Lee, Governor of Virginia and father of future Confederate General Robert E. Lee. Capitalizing on an opportunity to serve his country and make a name for himself, William used his family's well-established connections to obtain the rank of an officer in an infantry division.

Becoming a soldier was a way for William to prove himself worthy of being a "child of the revolution." In the military, he would distinguish himself as a General during the "Indian Wars" such as at Tippecanoe (hence his campaign slogan of "Tippecanoe and Tyler, too") and during the War of 1812. Moreover, in his political career, William would distinguish himself as Governor of the Indiana Territory and Superintendent of Indian affairs; U. S. congressman from Ohio; Ohio State and U. S. Senator; U.S. Minister to Columbia; and President of the United States.

Implicitly, the memory challenged Harrison to examine the lasting effects of the Revolutionary War on his life and to contemplate fundamental questions such as: Will I measure up to my revolutionary forefathers? What direction should my life take? What profession should I pursue? Will I leave an important historical legacy as did my father? What do I owe the future of my country? In sum, the memory—and Harrison's other reminiscences of his childhood—offer an image of him as a charter member of the Revolutionary generation who roamed across the Virginia landscape with famous figures such as Benedict Arnold, George Washington, Benjamin Rush, Patrick Henry, James Madison and Henry Lee.

Memory Two: "A Child of Caution"

After the Revolutionary War, William recalled that at the invitation of his father, a British aristocrat visited the Harrison estate at Berkeley. The nobleman remarked that the exteriors of the Virginia plantation were the equal of those in Britain, but that the interiors were void of paintings and decorations. His father, Colonel Benjamin Harrison replied, "I can account for my paintings and decorations, sir, your soldiers burned them in my backyard."
—*William Henry Harrison* by Gail Collins, page 11.

The memory represents more than a sarcastic quip. The fact that it was one of Harrison's earliest memories suggests that the beliefs and feelings contained within it reflected important perceptions he had of his father. The comment may have revealed the enduring emotional impact that traumatic events from the Revolutionary War continued to exert on both William and his father. The memory memorialized his father's underlying regret, anger and resentment at the British for making him and his family a casualty of the war.

The traumatic events to which his father responded in the memory may have reflected William's own sense of personal grievance at being wronged by the British. Biographer Robert Owens stated, "As the son of a hero of the American Revolution, William Harrison entertained a lifelong suspicion of British motives, policy, and even morality." Moreover, when he was almost 60, William Harrison described England as "Our ancient if not our natural enemy."

Perhaps William sensed that he was like his father, not just because they shared similar feelings about the British, but because they both shared a cautious communication style. For example, to avoid openly hurting the feelings of the English nobleman, Colonel Harrison suppressed his still raw hostile feelings and expressed himself in a more restrained manner to avoid friction or controversy. Similarly, Harrison once stated, "To Englishmen life is a topic, not an activity." This observational comment may have expressed Harrison's underlying condescension for the British: they were "all talk and no action," as opposed to Americans, who were spontaneous and action-oriented. A more calculated and deliberate communication style would help Harrison in his administrative role—assigned to him by Presidents John Adams and Thomas Jefferson—to secure as much territorial land from Native-Americans as possible. He did this in his role as Superintendant of Indian Affairs and later in his role as U.S. Minister to Bolivia.

Like his father, William may have stoked other personal resentments and injustices. For example, he was the last child in a family of three boys and four girls. In the 18th century, in the case of death, control of the plantation went to the first-born son, so William could not inherit any money from the family estate. By the time he was born, the family fortune had diminished and while his brothers were educated at William and Mary, William was educated at a second-rate school, by the standards of the Virginia elite. In addition, William's father expected him to pursue a career in medicine, one that could provide a reasonable income and did not require an expensive apprenticeship at the time. According to biographer Hendrick Booraem, "It is not unreasonable to suppose William compared his opportunities with those given to his older brothers before the war and realized the comparative shabbiness of his treatment." In this regard, William may have experienced resentment at being manipulated by his father and denied the right to pursue a profession of his own choosing.

At the beginning of his military career (1792) Ensign Harrison's commanding officer, General James Wilkinson, ordered that any soldier found intoxicated outside the walls of Fort Washington in Ohio receive 50 lashes. Following orders, Harrison applied the 50 lashes to the first offender and ten to the offender's protesting friend. In fact, the first offender was a civilian employee and he promptly filed a complaint with the civilian authorities. Harrison was arrested by a local deputy but intervention by General Wilkinson led to his release after spending one night in a civilian jail. General Wilkinson sent an account of the embarrassing incident to President Washington to gain his approval that the one night Harrison spent in jail—for what Harrison must have perceived as an injustice—would be the full extent of the punishment. According to General Wilkinson, Ensign Harrison was "One of the best disposed, most promising young Gentlemen in the Army." To add insult to injury, one of the civilian authorities in the case against Harrison was Judge John Cleves Symmes—who would later become Harrison's father-in-law!

 Another regret or disappointment from his youth (1794) involved an early romance with Hetty Morris, daughter of Robert Morris, who was known as the "Financier of the Revolution." In a letter to one of his brothers, Harrison indicated that it would be "humiliating" but he would stop courting Hetty if someone else came along with more prestigious social status: "I love her so ardently, I would forgo my own happiness forever to contribute to hers." Nevertheless, Harrison's status as a lowly officer and his limited financial resources prevented the courtship from going any further.

A memory of his father's lingering resentment of the losses they suffered at the hands of the British—embodied in the sarcastic comment, "I can account for my paintings and decorations, sir, your soldiers burned them in my backyard"—may have provoked Harrison to wonder whether he could let go of his own resentments; or whether he would dwell on past injustices and develop a sense of victimization. Perhaps Harrison's sensitivity about being wronged led to a zealousness when he felt denied. For example, Harrison may have believed that because of his service and contributions to America he was entitled to privileged treatment. The extent to which he may have exploited the sense of being wronged or victimized was revealed in a quote by President John Quincy Adams: "The greatest beggar and the most troublesome of all the office seekers during my Administration was General Harrison."

However, Harrison learned to move beyond his resentments and cultivated an agreeable, self-effacing manner. For example, Harrison was described by Reverend Timothy Fint, a friend of Harrison's from Ohio, as "urbane, hospitable, kind and utterly unpretentious." Soldiers who served under his command remembered him as a considerate commander who took an interest in their problems. Harrison wrote a letter in which he commented, "I prepared my mind to encounter with cheerfulness anything which the obligations of duty required me to perform." Harrison's self-effacing manner was evident from another comment he made about himself: "Some folks are silly enough to have formed a plan to make a President of the United States out of this Clerk and Clodhopper."

Harrison's father's carefully controlled response to the British nobleman served as a prototype for his son's carefully controlled responses during the 1840 Presidential campaign. For example, during the campaign, Harrison avoided mentioning contentious and polarizing subjects such as slavery; admitting Texas for statehood; or specifying how he would deal with the aftermath of the economic Panic of 1837. Harrison recognized the importance of fashioning his statements so they would not alienate the public. Accordingly, he offered the promise and hope of Revolutionary ideals without identifying specific policies. In fact, some opponents called him "General Mum" because of his reluctance to speak out on controversial issues. Moreover, poet Ralph Waldo Emerson remarked, "General Harrison is neither Whig nor Tory but the Indignation President."

Mass rallies, and slogans or jingoisms such as "Tippecanoe and Tyler, Too" became the underpinnings of his Whig campaign. Harrison's Democratic opposition attempted to undermine his credibility with comments such as: "Give him a barrel of hard cider and settle a pension of $2,000 a year on him and, my word for it, he will sit the remainder of his days in a log cabin by the side of a sea coal fire, and study moral philosophy." Harrison responded by running a "log cabin and hard cider" campaign where rallies were held in log cabins and hard cider was served in generous portions to potential voters. Of course, Harrison did not grow up in a log cabin—he was part of Virginia's elite class—he grew up in a mansion and had a dislike for drinking alcohol. But the marketing campaign capitalized on Harrison's affability and humility and 80.2% of the voters turned out to elect him—a record that remains to this day! Harrison's opponent, Martin Van Buren was characterized as an effete snob while Harrison was depicted as the man with the "common touch."

Harrison set the tone for the modern politician—the charmer with the common touch. He was just the type of "grass roots" leader America needed to recast its image as a nation where, according to Harrison, "the rich get richer and the poor get poorer." Harrison became the first presidential candidate to personally campaign for the job. As a politician, Harrison needed to calculate the consequences of his actions and the memory provided him with a dose of needed perspective. The disastrous events that led to his father's lingering resentment could happen again, albeit in a different context, so the memory helped Harrison to hope for the best and prepare for the worst.

Harrison may have also learned from the memory that for his father, and in life, there were no completely satisfying endings—problems followed successes. This lesson would serve him well in a long and distinguished career in which he did not become president until age 67—at the time, the oldest President to hold office. Despite his many accomplishments, Harrison's life, as was his father's, was marked by disappointments and personal tragedies. For example, William and his wife, Anna, had ten children, six of whom did not survive past childhood. In addition, twice Harrison ran unsuccessfully for office in Ohio as a U.S. Senator; lost a bid as Governor of Ohio; lost out to John C. Calhoun for the office of Secretary of War in the administration of President James Monroe; and prior to the 1840 Presidential campaign his financial situation was so dire that he felt pressured to obtain a job as a records clerk for the county court to earn extra money.

The financial burdens created by the ransacking of the Harrison estate were inextricably linked to Colonel Harrison's subsequent struggles to support his family. In the aftermath, Colonel Harrison attempted to maintain the living conditions to which he and his family had become accustomed—which was untenable given the fiscal changes in his life. William had much to learn from a memory that depicted his father's economic misfortune—from comprehending its scope to whether his father could have done something different to avoid the dire monetary results that followed.

Perhaps Harrison wondered if he, too, would experience the financially difficulties that plagued his father. Colonel Harrison's precarious financial status would actually become a preview of how William spent much of his life struggling to support his own large family. President John Quincy Adams remarked, Harrison's "thirst for lucrative office is absolutely rabid, Vice-president, major-general of the Army, Minister to Columbia—for each of these places he has been this very session as hot in pursuit as a hound on the scent of a hare." In fact, Harrison found himself in debt throughout his life and once wrote a friend, "My great object is to save a little money."

Philosopher George Santayana claimed that "those who cannot remember the past are condemned to repeat it," implying that memory can help to prevent the repetition of a problem. In recalling this memory, Harrison may have been trying to immunize himself against the fear of financial vulnerability—that ultimately he could lose everything that he now possessed—as did his father. Unfortunately for Harrison, the end was in the beginning: he died nearly penniless. Hence, Judge Symme's worst fear that his son-in-law would not be able to support his daughter had come true. Even though William Henry Harrison died after only thirty-one days in office, Congress voted to provide his wife the equivalent of one year of Harrison's Presidential salary—$25,000. In part, Anna Harrison used this money to pay off her husband's considerable debt.

Memory Three: "A Child of Tenacity"

In 1795, William Harrison courted Anna Symmes. When William asked her father for Anna's hand in marriage, the Judge asked him, "How do you propose to support my daughter?" Harrison responded, "By my sword and my right hand, sir!"
> —*William Henry Harrison*, by Henry Green, page 62

As previously mentioned, Anna's father, Judge John Cleves Symmes, was one of the civilian judges who presided in a case in which Ensign Harrison was arrested for administering 50 lashes to an intoxicated individual at Fort Washington. The involvement of Judge Symmes may or may not have impacted his subsequent decision to disapprove of the marriage between his daughter and William. It is assumed that he felt such a marriage was not in his daughter's best interests because of William's poor financial prospects; and because he wanted to prevent her from experiencing the many hardships and dangers of Army life.

In recounting the authenticity of this memory and the events related to it, biographer Gail Collins stated, "Exactly how the Harrisons were married is subject to debate. Some stories suggest that the couple gathered with friends on a day when the Colonel was out of town and pulled off a modified elopement, with a ceremony at the home of a friend. Other versions say that Anna was married in her own house, and that her father was present but stalked off in the middle of the ceremony."

Regardless of the exact circumstances, it is evident that Harrison felt Judge Symmes underestimated him and found him lacking in his chances for future success. Soon after the marriage, his father-in-law described Harrison to a friend, "He can neither bleed, plead, nor preach, [that is, be a doctor, lawyer nor minister] and if he could plow I should be satisfied." Harrison's perception of being underestimated would influence his responses to future challenges, no matter what form they took—an underestimation of his abilities, or an election lost—he would be prepared to face and overcome any challenge with which he was confronted.

William's response to his future father-in-law as to how he would protect his wife, "By my sword and my right hand, sir!" indicated that he was eager to prove he had more potential than Judge Symmes or others gave him credit for; and that he was ready to face any subsequent challenge with determination and resolve. The memory served to affirm that William Henry Harrison would be a good provider—not because of his financial resources, but because of his determination—especially compared to his more financially well-off counterparts. He would defy the odds—like the Revolutionary generation of which he was a part—and transform himself into someone worthy of the Judge's support and respect.

Referring to a "sword" provided a powerful image of Harrison poised as a wily, able-handed warrior prepared to "slash" any obstacle in his way. An image of himself as a "knight in shining armor" inspired him to have confidence in himself, to be self-reliant and not to let someone else's underestimation of him extinguish his dream of a promising future. In his career as a soldier and a General, when William Harrison acted he made sure he had a sword in his hand.

Harrison's boldness was on display in 1794 at the Battle of Fallen Timbers. As a Lieutenant under the direction of Major General "Mad" Anthony Wayne, Harrison was responsible for protecting Fort Washington from a large-scale attack by Native American forces. Harrison fought in the battle and received an official commendation from General Wayne for his valor: "I must add the name of my faithful and gallant Aide-de-Camp, Lieutenant Harrison, who rendered the most essential service by communicating my orders in every direction, and by his conduct and bravery in exciting the troops to press for victory." In the Battle of Fallen Timbers, Harrison acquitted himself well, thus earning the unwavering support of General Wayne and proving the implied message in the memory: No matter the challenge, Harrison would prevail, stand out from the rest and make a name for himself.

On becoming a General, other authorities shared a similar assessment of Harrison's bravery and resolve: In1814, Governor Isaac Shelby of Kentucky remarked, "I believe him to be one of the finest military characters I ever knew; and, in addition to this, he is capable of making greater personal exertions than any officer with whom I have ever served." Harrison armed himself with a memory that provided the confidence he needed to display an assertive and self-possessed manner; a manner that would help to prevent others (like Judge Symmes) from underestimating his worth. Perhaps the unswerving self-confidence that was inspired by the memory contributed to the high regard in which Harrison was held during his military career.

The impact of the memory was evident in Harrison's heightened sense of self-assuredness. The more self-assured he was, the more prepared he would be for whatever lay ahead. Harrison once wrote a letter in which he said, "While I wear [an officer's] sword & the livery of my country I will not disgrace them by owning myself inferior to any person." His self-assuredness may have been a key to his revolutionary appeal in the 1840 Presidential election. Harrison made the common man feel better about himself because he felt so positive in his own chances—and America's—for future success.

Harrison's self-assuredness was also evident in the performance of his duties as U.S. Ambassador to Columbia. Appointed by John Quincy Adams in 1828, Harrison believed that the U.S. needed to make Columbia safe for democracy. There is a sense that Harrison believed so passionately in his views of the supremacy of the American form of government that he saw fit to lecture Columbia's ruler, Simon Bolivar. In a letter to Bolivar, Harrison asked, "Are you willing that your name should descend to posterity amongst the mass of those whose fame has been derived from shedding human blood, without a single advantage to the human race? Or shall it be united to that of Washington as the founder and the father of a great and happy people?" In addition, Harrison stated in the letter, "The strongest of all government is that which is most free."

In part, Harrison's comments were a reaction to Bolivar's increasing use of dictatorial powers to thwart an insurrection. Harrison believed that these authoritarian measures were antithetical to American values. From Harrison's point of view, if Bolivar felt offended at being lectured, he was only saying the right thing and for the right reasons, and if the comments were delivered with the sharpness of a "sword" then he should be admired for summoning America's grander values. Nevertheless, some Columbian officials took offense at what they viewed as Harrison siding with the opposition (to President Bolivar) and planned to expel him from the ambassadorship. When Andrew Jackson became President, Harrison was recalled from his post so Jackson could appoint his own "hand-picked" ambassador to Columbia.

Harrison's comments to Bolivar may have been rooted in a memory in which he learned the importance of self-assertion and capitalizing on the circumstances of the moment. If others viewed this self-confidence as showmanship or depicting a vainglorious personality, Harrison saw himself as holding deep personal convictions and democratic values. Clearly, this was not the view of Senator John C. Calhoun of South Carolina who in 1841 stated, "As unconscious as a child of his difficulties and those of his country, he seems to enjoy his election as a mere affair for personal vanity. It is really distressing to see him."

Calhoun's evaluation seemed inaccurate. Even if the memory contributed to an exaggerated belief in his own strengths and accomplishments, most perceived Harrison as approachable and good-natured as opposed to arrogant and condescending. Nevertheless, a sense of self-importance and entitlement may have led to at least one decision of dubious merit: fathering six children by one of his slaves named Dilsia. Historian Kenneth Robert Janken noted that the mother of Walter Francis White, a civil rights leader, vouched for the authenticity of this claim.
In addition to being remembered for having the shortest Presidential time in office—31 days—Harrison is also remembered for having the longest Inaugural Address on record—one hour and forty-five minutes. Harrison delivered the address, edited by Daniel Webster,

on a cold and rainy day without wearing an overcoat or gloves. He contracted pneumonia and died one month later.

During the1840 presidential campaign Harrison was pilloried for being a "sham hero" chided as "Granny Harrison the petticoat general" (because he was the oldest man ever to seek the presidency) and mocked as a "superannuated and pitiable dotard." A Philadelphia newspaper remarked, "General Harrison was always a coward, always a foe to the people, always as rapacious as Verres and as infamous as Arnold. We know not whether most to scorn his imbecility, to hate his principles, or wonder at his impudent effrontery." One can only imagine how difficult it must have been to be compared to Benedict Arnold—the devil incarnate in his first memory!

In part, to offset this negative image, Harrison was determined to reestablish the self-assured, vital and totally in-charge of himself characterization that was depicted in the memory. By delivering a long inaugural address—and doing so without protective apparel—Harrison tried to prove to the nation—as he tried to prove to Judge Symmes in the memory—that he was strong, resilient, determined, and the right person to "weather any storm."

Summary

Throughout his career, Harrison lived up to the promise of the title he assigned to himself in Memory One, "a Child of the Revolution." He distinguished himself as a soldier, general, congressman, governor, senator and ambassador. But for all of his accomplishments, the Presidency must have seemed like the best opportunity for Harrison to seal his legacy and make his presence felt with compelling force. This was the position he felt destined to assume since he was a nine-year-old boy growing up in Virginia. Now Harrison's legacy as President would be considered not only inevitable, but inarguable. But it wasn't to be. Harrison died before he had a chance to establish his legacy as President.

The belief that "life is unfair" united the first two memories. Memory Three foreshadowed how Harrison would try to combat this belief—he would deal with each challenge life delivered with the best effort of which he was capable. He would use his sword to cut through all the resentments, all the unfairness and distinguish himself as a patriotic American that served his country and left a formidable legacy. Harrison lost so many elections and suffered so many disappointments and tragedies that resentment could easily have become the core of his identity. But he never gave up; and in his struggle to define himself and his legacy, he became President of the United States—the final act he needed to fulfill the promise contained in his first memory.

Together the three memories provided Harrison with a story of origin and a way to understand himself and the country he loved (Memory One); a perspective of caution and restraint (Memory Two); and a willingness to act coupled with a determination to overcome all obstacles (Memory Three). Each memory provided an indispensable clue to Harrison's character.

To the best of his ability, Harrison tried to reconcile the positive and negative influences of each memory. On the positive side, inspired by Memory One, Harrison's love of country was unwavering. He was the General responsible for the defeat of the Shawnee at Tippecanoe, and at the Battle of Thames he led troops against a British and Native-American coalition that included the legendary leader Tecumseh. His efforts as Governor of the Northwest Territory were critical in purchasing more than 50 million acres—at pennies per acre—of Native-American land. On the negative side, Memory One may have contributed to a racially-biased perspective and an intolerance for contrary viewpoints. This was the case in Harrison's dealings with Native Americans in which his negotiation strategy was rooted in a proud nationalism that equated the greater good with whatever benefited America.

Guided by Memory Two, Harrison developed a cautious, calculating and restrained manner that helped him to out-think his adversaries; on the negative side, the memory may have contributed toward an over-cautiousness that sometimes led to inaction in the face of conflict. This was the case in the campaign of 1840 in which Harrison was all too eager to insulate himself against the possibility of disagreement or controversy.

Inspired by Memory Three, Harrison developed the belief that he could overcome any challenge with a confident and determined manner; on the negative side, the memory may have predisposed him toward a sense of bravado and an off-putting air of superiority. This was the case in Columbia where Ambassador Harrison was determined to spread democracy and impose American values in a country where some viewed his efforts as condescending and self-righteous.

Throughout his long career, we see the profound impact of the three memories and the ways in which they enabled Harrison to acknowledge the contradictions in his own personality. The last words spoken by Harrison were directed to his doctor, probably consciously intended for Vice-President John Tyler, and perhaps unconsciously a manifestation of his enigmatic style (Memory Two) while at the same time appearing sincere and passionate (Memory Three): "Sir, I wish you to understand the true principles of the government. I wish them carried out. I ask nothing more."

Bibliography

Booraem, Hendrick. A Child of the Revolution: William Henry Harrison and His World, 1773–1798. Kent State University Press: Kent, Ohio, 2012.
> *This detailed, interesting and insightful book describes Harrison's early life from a psychological perspective.*

Collins, Gail. William Henry Harrison. Times Books: Henry Holt and Company, New York, 2012.
> *A balanced, incisive examination of Harrison's entire life.*

Cleaves, Freeman. Old Tippecanoe. Newtown, Connecticut: American Political Biography Press, 1990.

Goebel, Dorothy Burne. William Henry Harrison. Indianapolis: Historical Bureau of the Indiana Library and Historical Department, 1926.

Green, James. William Henry Harrison His Life and Times. Garrett and Massie Inc., Richmond, Virginia, 1941.

Anderson, Robert . The Log-Cabin Campaign. Westport, Connecticut: Greenwood Press, 1977.

Owens, Robert. Mr. Jefferson's hammer: William Henry Harrison and the Origins of American Indian Policy. University of Oklahoma press: Norman, 2007.

Schlesinger , Arthur (editor). The Election of 1840 and the Harrison/Tyler Administrations. Philadelphia: Mason Crest Publishers, 2003.

Zachary Taylor

President of the United States
March 1849 – July 1850

Memory One: "Mrs. Chenoweth"

A nearby neighbor, the irrepressible Mrs. Chenoweth, often startled and amused Zachary and his peers by removing her headgear and displaying her bald head, which was described as peeled like an onion by the Indians' bluntest scalping knife—and shorn of her beautiful hair.

—*Zachary Taylor*, by John S. D. Eisenhower[1] page 2.

Zachary Taylor was born in Orange County, Virginia in 1784. His father, Richard Taylor served as a lieutenant colonel in the American Revolution. In 1785, his family moved to the unsettled frontier in the state of Kentucky, a few miles from modern day Louisville. Young Zachary grew up in a wilderness atmosphere where danger was the norm. According to biographer Holman Hamilton, residents lived in fear of attacks by Native Americans:

> *The village proper and its immediate environs could boast of only one hundred inhabitants who had cleared and cultivated garden-spots around their humble cabins ... All else was the primeval forest, with panthers and bears and wolves and wildcats.*

Taylor experienced other compelling dangers of frontier life such as volatile weather, susceptibility to disease, demanding physical challenges in cultivating the land; and, in 1792, his father, Colonel Richard Taylor was wounded during a skirmish with the Native Americans of Little Turtle. One of Taylor's first teachers, Elisha Ayer, described an ominous picture of young Zachary's surroundings:

---

[1] John S. D. Eisenhower is the brother of President Dwight D. Eisenhower.

> *The Kentuckians were then a warlike and chivalrous people and they were often engaged in offensive or defensive skirmishes with the Indians. A number [of Indians] were known to be in the woods not far distant from the school-house, and, on one occasion, one of them was shot, wearing a British uniform. In their hostility to the Americans, they were encouraged and sustained by the British authorities on the Northern frontier. There was a Mr. Whetsel, in the neighborhood of the school, who, having been once chased by three or four Indians, loaded his rifle while running, and successively shot them all.*

After thinking about an image of Mrs. Chenoweth being "scalped"—or Mr. Whetsel being chased—perhaps the harshness, privations and risks Taylor faced on a daily basis did not seem so severe to him. In using humor to defuse tension, perhaps Mrs. Chenoweth inspired Taylor to laugh at his own fear of danger, or at least not to take the fear so seriously. Mrs. Chenoweth's tone was light and in her bemusement she seemed to be unfazed by her appearance. The narrative allowed Taylor to face, undeterred, a dangerous and unforgiving world. For example, in 1837, Taylor fought the Seminoles at the Battle of Okeechobee. Along with his men, he advanced through the swamps, with muck up to his waist; and, as a result, was given the nickname "Old Rough and Ready."

Objectively, the memory described a down-to-earth lady who disregarded conventional niceties. Taylor identified with Mrs. Chenoweth's plight, her lack of pretense and her idiosyncratic presentation. Unconcerned by what others may have thought of her, Mrs. Chenoweth gained self-respect and confidence by embracing her tainted identity and physical peculiarities. To her credit, she confronted her past and did not put on airs. Her example may have been an important lesson in Taylor's life, challenging him to be authentic—true to himself.

Taylor was unpretentious. He rarely combed his hair or wore an officer's uniform; and as a General he dressed in a manner that did not reflect his elevated status. Typically, being dressed in uniform consisted of baggy cotton pants, a plain coat bearing no insignia, and a farmer's wide-brimmed straw hat. Unlike George Washington or Andrew Jackson, Taylor did not look like a strong or inspiring leader. A lieutenant described him as being, "short and very heavy ... wears an old oil cloth cap, a dusty green coat, a frightful pair of trousers and on horseback looks like a toad!"

In addition, like Mrs. Chenoweth, Taylor was idiosyncratic. As president, his odd informality often surprised White House visitors. For example, visitors could see Taylor's horse, Old Whitey, grazing on the White House lawn! Moreover, according to biographer Robin Doak, "Some found Taylor spattered with tobacco juice that had dribbled from his mouth. The president was quite proud of his ability to spit tobacco juice accurately from several feet away." For visitors who may have found his behavior off-putting, or un-presidential, the following comment by Taylor no doubt confirmed their negative assessment: "I would be as happy in a cabin as in the White House."

In *The Complete Book of U.S. Presidents*, Taylor was described as:

> *... a disproportionate figure, with long, gangling arms, a thickly set torso, and short, bowed legs—He dressed sloppily, wearing whatever was most comfortable and walked or stood with one hand behind his back—He stammered occasionally and thought carefully before speaking.*

Clearly, Taylor's overall manner did not impress President James Polk, who wrote that Taylor was "uneducated, exceedingly ignorant of public affairs, and I should judge of very ordinary capacity."

Educator Horace Mann commented:

> *Taylor really is a most simple-minded old man. He has the least show or pretension about him of any man I ever saw; talks as artlessly as a child about affairs of state, and does not seem to pretend to a knowledge of anything of which he is ignorant. He is a remarkable man in some respects; and it is remarkable that such a man should be President of United States.*

The memory provided encouragement that one day Taylor, like Mrs. Chenoweth, would show his worthiness to individuals who regarded him in a diminished or compromised manner, as did James Polk and Horace Mann. This expectation sustained Taylor during times of self-doubt. Accordingly, the memory may have helped Taylor to better understand and process his own feelings of being different. Mrs. Chenoweth's quirkiness inspired Taylor to be more accepting of his own eccentricities without being ashamed of them. Perhaps Taylor thought that Mrs. Chenoweth's condition actually helped her to become stronger, braver and more capable of handling adversity. If so, Mrs. Chenoweth was viewed by Taylor as some kind of frontier heroine who taught him that he too could face adversities and become stronger, braver and more authentic in the process.

Taylor's identification with Mrs. Chenoweth found extension in his compassion for others, no matter their differences. He learned to lead not by outward appearance but by setting a good example and by demonstrating a lifelong habit of duty and responsibility to those who suffered. For example, at Fort Snelling, Taylor set up a school for Winnebago Native American children. In letters to friends and family, he criticized how the army handled Native American uprisings and blamed settlers, traders, and miners for fomenting difficulties with Native Americans. Over time, Taylor gained a reputation for fairness in administering Indian affairs.

Taylor's unorthodox and disheveled appearance portrayed him as an ordinary guy that exuded compassion for the common man. In turn, soldiers respected Taylor's concern for their welfare. In 1847 at the Battle of Buena Vista, General Taylor and 5,000 of his troops were surrounded by General Antonio Lopez de Santa Anna and an army of some 20,000 men. When it was suggested to Taylor that he should retreat to a better position, he replied, "No, we will decide the battle here! I will never, alive, leave my wounded behind."

In addition to his compassion toward the Native Americans and his own troops, Taylor exhibited compassion toward the enemies that he vanquished. In 1846, after four days of intensive fighting at the battle of Monterrey, the Mexicans called for a truce. In exchange for surrendering Monterrey, Taylor allowed the Mexican army to retreat with their firearms, with some of their artillery and ammunition; and he also agreed not to pursue the Mexicans for eight weeks. Taylor conceded that the terms were generous but he felt "it would be judicious to act with magnanimity toward a prostrate foe." In this case, Taylor's compassion was viewed by President James Polk as misguided, if not a capitulation, and as a result Polk gave General Winfield Scott the honor of attacking Mexico City, at which point Scott reassigned most of Taylor's troops to his command.

Taylor faced challenges on the home front as well. In 1820, two of his five daughters died of malaria. During the same period of time, his wife, Margaret became ill. She managed to recover, though her health was never the same. When his second-eldest daughter, Sarah, turned eighteen years old, she met Lieutenant Jefferson Davis (future President of the Confederacy) and became engaged. Taylor opposed their marriage, commenting: "I will be damned if another daughter of mine shall marry into the army—I know the family life of officers—I scarcely know my own children or they me."

Taylor's fear of danger to Sarah if she married someone in the army became a self-fulfilling prophecy, but not in the way Taylor had feared; in 1835, three months after Jefferson and Sarah were married, Sarah contracted malaria and died.

So although the tale of Mrs. Chenoweth may seem to have been just a humorous memory, it may have allowed Taylor to identify a traumatic event that he feared might actually happen to him. If you have ever "whistled in the dark," you will know that it is probably a combination of both. "Removing her headgear and exposing her bald head" was a way for Mrs. Chenoweth to respond to her anxieties and fears about her appearance by disavowing them and then projecting them onto others by startling and scaring them.

Taylor held onto a memory that provided him with the opportunity to master his own anxieties and fears regarding the real dangers he faced on the Kentucky frontier during the late18th century, and later as a General in the army.

Memory Two: "Cooling the Fires of Apprehension"

One day the niece of Zachary's mother—Sarah Taylor Woofolk—was "assisting" her aunt in molding bullets. In a ladle made of hard wood a coal of fire was placed, a piece of tallow was put on the coal and the lead put on to melt. Suddenly the cry Indians! Indians! was heard. In the excitement, Zachary's mother turned the melted lead over Sarah's hand. To her dying day her fingers were stiffened and crooked from the effect of the burn.

—Zachary Taylor: Soldier of the Republic,
by Holman Hamilton, page 30.

In recalling this incident, young Zachary may have imagined what he might do if attacked by an Indian or other such crisis. Would he scream and run away? Would he drop something as did his mother? Or would he face the danger in a stalwart and courageous manner? The process of asking these questions would have become a way for Taylor to anticipate his responses in stressful situations. In repeating or recalling this incident, Taylor would have felt active, willing and in control of the situation, instead of being passive or helpless. The anticipation of danger was something to be mastered through repetition.

The memory served to warn Taylor of crisis situations that he could expect and for which he could prepare. This advanced preparation might have been helpful to him when, according to biographer Hamilton Holman, "tradition has it that a party of children, of whom Zachary Taylor was one, was attacked by savages." Whereas this "attack" on young Zachary may have been apocryphal, it clearly illuminated the conflicted frame of mind in which Taylor operated. In fact, as noted previously, when Taylor was a boy his father was wounded in a battle with Native Americans. Additionally, when he was a young soldier, Taylor's brother William was killed when a contingent of Chickasaws attacked Fort Pickering in 1808.

In recalling his cousin being scalded, Taylor found tangible form for his sense of impending danger. This may have inspired him to keep his wits about him and maintain his composure under pressure. For example, in the war of 1812, Chief Tecumseh led the Shawnee

Warriors in an attack against Fort Harrison. Taylor's men were outnumbered ten-to-one and when the Shawnees hurled burning torches into a supply facility, the situation seemed dire. Many soldiers panicked and some even deserted. Despite the pressure, Taylor galvanized his remaining men and helped them to extinguish the fire, thus preventing the attackers from penetrating the Fort.

In a report about the incident Taylor wrote, "What from the raging of the fire, the yelling and howling of several hundred Indians, the cries of nine women and children—I can assure you that my feelings were very unpleasant." Armed with a memory that inoculated him against impending danger, Taylor saved Fort Harrison; and President James Madison promoted the twenty-seven-year-old Taylor to Brevet Major. Taylor was the first soldier to be given this title, created by Congress "to reward heroism."

Determined not to be overwhelmed by his anticipatory anxiety, Taylor concealed his fear of danger behind a manifest presentation of fearlessness that served to deny the fear that likely existed within him. In the presidential election of 1848, many voters believed that the nation was hopelessly divided and that a fearless and unpretentious person such as General Zachary Taylor could manage the divisiveness without leading the country into a Civil War. Taylor was nominated by the Whig party to run for president with Millard Fillmore as Vice President. Voters supported Taylor because, as Abraham Lincoln, who had served under Captain Zachary Taylor in the Blackhawk War, stated:

> *Taylor was never beaten, and he never retreated; and yet in all he triumphed; but in all he seems rather to have conquered by the exercise of a sober and steady judgment, coupled with a dogged incapacity to understand that defeat was possible. His rarest military trait was a combination of negatives—absence of excitement and absence of fear. He could not be flurried, and he could not be scared.*

To Lincoln, what appeared to be an absence of excitement and fear was actually Taylor protecting himself from the dangerous implications of an early frightening memory from his youth and provide him with strength and courage. In 1846, U.S. and Mexican armies met at a small lake called Palo Alto. In this battle, Taylor's soldiers were outnumbered three-to-one. During one of the fierce skirmishes, Mexican General Arista stayed in his tent, while General Taylor rode his horse, "Old Whitey" onto the battlefield. One soldier wrote that Taylor rallied his men "in the thickest of the fight, with his sword drawn, while the cannonballs were rattling around him."

Although some criticized Taylor's actions as reckless and foolhardy, Lieutenant Ulysses S. Grant was impressed with what he thought was Taylor's grace under pressure: "No soldier could face either danger or responsibility more calmly then he—these are qualities more rarely found than genius or physical courage." Subsequently, a gold medal was specifically designed for Taylor and Congress passed a resolution thanking Taylor and his men "for the fortitude, skill, enterprise and courage, which have distinguished the recent brilliant operations on the Rio Grande."

When Taylor was inaugurated in 1849, two western territories, California and New Mexico, requested statehood. Taylor had owned slaves throughout his adult life, but he believed that California and New Mexico should be admitted as free states. In Congress, David Wilmot attached an amendment that prohibited slavery in California, and in all territories that the United States acquired after the Mexican war. This was known as the Wilmot Proviso and Taylor supported it. A pro-slavery Texas delegation threatened secession, but Taylor demonstrated the same fearlessness under pressure that he showed in battle. He responded to the delegation by admonishing them:

> *If it becomes necessary I'll take command of the army myself and if you are taken in rebellion against the Union I will hang you with less reluctance than I hanged deserters and spies in Mexico.*

When the Texas delegation threatened secession, perhaps Taylor remembered an important lesson from the memory: Prepare for danger before it happens. Taylor's resolute response to the delegation helped to prevent a civil war from breaking out during his administration. If not for a presidency that lasted only sixteen months—before Taylor died of a cholera outbreak in 1850—Taylor's unpretentious, straightforward and fearless leadership style might have had a significant impact on healing some of the deep divisions within the United States.

As Senator Thomas Hart Benton remarked after Taylor's death:

> *His death was a public calamity. No man could have been more devoted to the Union or more opposed to the slavery agitation, and his position as a Southern man and a slave-holder, his military reputation and his election by a majority of the people of the states would have given him a power in the settlement of these questions which no President without these qualifications would have possessed.*

Of course, there is no way to know what might have happened if Taylor had actually completed his term. However, during his sixteen months in office, Taylor signed the Clayton-Bulwer Treaty between Great Britain and the United States (1850). This treaty provided the United States with fair and equal access to any Central American canals built in the future. As a result, the United States secured an important transportation route, and eventually the Panama Canal was opened in 1914. The English diplomat who helped to negotiate the treaty, Sir Henry Bulwer, described Taylor in the following manner:

> *His intentions were always good; his word could always be relied upon; his manners were downright, simple, straightforward; his name was popular throughout the Union, and he died almost universally respected and lamented.*

Memory Three: "Diving into Uncertain Waters"

When but 17 years old Zachary Taylor swam across the Ohio River from the Kentucky to the Indiana Shore, in the month of March, when the river was filled with floating ice, which is a feat far surpassing in danger and difficulty the farfamed exploit of swimming the Hellespont.

Many other well attested memories are related of his daring adventures, and his love of bold and dangerous exploits.
—*The Life of Major General Zachary Taylor*, by Henry Montgomery, e-book page 42/3930.

The previous memories involving Mrs. Chenoweth and Taylor's cousin focused on the inherent dangers of living a frontier life and what could happen. Memory Three focuses on his refusal to be intimidated by any obstacle or danger the frontier might present. Recalling the incident may have been a way for Taylor to elevate his mood—providing him with a message of hope in a world full of daunting challenges.

The other "well attested memories" that the biographer, Montgomery, made reference to, reflected experiences in which Taylor sought out challenging adventures in the wilderness. In these solitary excursions, Taylor saw himself as a lone wolf "roaming through forests and over boundless prairies." In blazing a path through the wilderness—by himself—Taylor was desensitizing himself to the dangers of the wild. As a result, he was more prepared to take on other "hazardous enterprises" in the future.

In the memory, Taylor did not receive help from others in swimming across the river. This can be viewed as a declaration of his independence and self-sufficiency. Swimming across the channel was less about winning a contest and more about how Taylor wanted to live his life—by doing something nobody else would try, doing it on his terms and doing it alone. From early on, Taylor linked his self-image to his solitude, to his tenacity and to his sense of adventure. Taylor's toughest competitor was himself, and in controlling himself he was trying to control his fate.

Taylor's unabashedly "down to earth" manner of dressing can be viewed as an enactment of something that a General or President was not supposed to do. But Taylor did it because that was his way of operating on his own terms. He did not submit to conventional ways, just as he did not submit to his fear of danger, he would gain the advantage by using his strengths, such as individuality and resourcefulness, rather than follow established conventions.

Perhaps when Taylor attained the rank of General, or when he was elected President, he remembered swimming across the river and thought about the parallels between his preference for solitude and the responsibilities of his lofty position. Dwight David Eisenhower compared the presidency to a field of battle:

> *The nakedness of the battlefield when the soldier is all alone in the smoke and the clamor and the terror of war is comparable to the loneliness—at times—of the presidency. These are the times when one man must conscientiously, deliberately, prayerfully scrutinize every argument, every proposal, every prediction, every alternative, every probable outcome of his action and then—all alone—make his decision.*

In this regard, the message of the memory seemed right on the mark, if a seventeen-year-old could swim across a river filled with floating ice, then a General Taylor or a President Taylor could make a difficult decision—all alone—and achieve a successful outcome.

In swimming across the icy river, Taylor demonstrated self-reliance and a preference for doing things in a non-conventional way. These characteristics were evident during the 1848 presidential campaign in which Taylor may have appeared to some voters as a "fish out of water." For example, prior to 1848, Taylor had never cast a ballot in a presidential election and he was the first president to be elected without having held a previous political office. Whatever his political views may have been, Taylor did not feel bound by the convention of voting or of holding a political office and likely never gave thought to running for the presidency.

Additionally, Taylor saw himself as a different kind of presidential candidate who was not bound by the formality of party principles or ideology. As a result, he did not declare himself as a member of the Whig party until six weeks before the Whig national convention. When he did affiliate with the party, Taylor avoided adopting the official party line on controversial issues such as the tariff and allowing slavery to spread into territories that were captured during the Mexican War. Taylor maintained, "I am a Whig, but not an ultra Whig" and he declared, "If elected I would not be the mere president of a party, I would endeavor to act independent of party domination and should feel bound to administer the Government untrammeled by party schemes."

After he was elected President, Taylor demonstrated the same independence that he displayed as a seventeen-year-old in swimming across the river. For example, he eschewed the traditional patronage system and selected candidates for governmental positions based on merit. In this case, members of his own Whig party criticized Taylor for not following the conventional practice of appointing members of his own party to office.

In another example, Taylor did not actively seek the partnership of fellow Whig Henry Clay (Senator from Kentucky and majority leader in the Senate) regarding the issue of which territories applying for statehood would be admitted as slave states. Taylor was a slaveholder, as was Clay, but they both believed that slavery should be limited to the areas in which it was already practiced and not extended to new territories. But instead of viewing Clay as a potential ally, Taylor seemed to view him as a rival, and for the most part they operated independently. In this case, Taylor's preference for managing his affairs on his own prevented him from gaining the internal support that was necessary in order to achieve his administration's goals. Taylor's "singular" political style prompted Senator Clay to comment:

> *I have never before seen such an Administration. There is very little cooperation or concord between the two ends of the avenue. There is not, I believe, a prominent Whig in either House that has any confidential intercourse with the Executive.*

Southern states felt betrayed by Taylor's departure from the southern orthodoxy on the expansion of slavery and threatened to secede from the Union. Taylor opposed the Compromise of 1850, which would allow territories taken in the Mexican-American war to determine by popular sovereignty whether to allow slavery or not. Taylor wanted all new territories to be free. Here he was once again "swimming upstream"—playing the unexpected "Northern Role" rather than the expected role of a "Southern partisan."

Without support from key congressmen or senators, Taylor's independent "I do it my way" posture left the congress hopelessly deadlocked on the issue of the expansion of slavery. Taylor was ready to veto the Compromise if it passed through Congress; but he came down with acute gastroenteritis on July 4, 1850 and died a week later. Taylor's untimely death prevented him from fully utilizing the "free-form strategy" that enabled him to swim the ice-filled channel and that he had hoped would unify the country.

In the memory, Taylor's preference to "do it alone and do it his way" was so compelling that it may have contributed in part to his death. The cholera epidemic that started in late 1848 was extensively reported in the Washington newspapers. Washingtonians were advised to avoid drinking milk, refrain from drinking large quantities of water and admonished to not eat raw fruits and vegetables. Insistent on doing things his own way, Taylor did not heed the warnings. One can only imagine Taylor saying to himself, "Why should I? Because the newspapers want me to? Because the doctors want me to?" Taylor remained unscripted to the end. After returning home that afternoon on July 4, 1850, in the midst of a heat wave, Taylor ate cherries and raw vegetables and drank a large quantity of iced milk. By evening, "Old Rough and Ready" was stricken with cholera.

Just as he was reluctant to toe the party line, Taylor was reluctant to follow reasonable health suggestions. He may have succeeded in proving to others that he was his own man, a lone wolf, someone who was not cowed by battlefield enemies or by party elites; but, in the end, he never really proved it to himself. Simply being himself was dangerous.

Summary

These memories provide the most in-depth look at Taylor's character and reveal important lessons he learned about managing his emotions, such as how to cope with fear and anxiety and how to be confident and resilient.

In the first memory, Taylor saw himself in Mrs. Chenoweth's idiosyncratic and authentic presentation—like her, he was unpretentious and down-to-earth. They both came from the frontier and harbored the same fear of danger. Just as Taylor's unconventional and informal manner made him popular with ordinary soldiers, Mrs. Chenoweth's unconventional and informal manner made her popular with young Zachary and his peers. When Taylor left the military to run for the presidency, he envisioned himself as a political outsider who placed the needs of the nation ahead of partisan politics. This perception of himself can be viewed as an approximation of his perception of Mrs. Chenoweth—one who placed authenticity and spontaneous self-expression ahead of formalities and conventions.

The second memory is a brief examination of how Taylor's family struggled to survive the dangers of an unforgiving frontier life. Fearful and anxious that she was but a tomahawk assault away from tragedy, Young Zachary's mother dropped her ladle when "suddenly she heard the cry of Indians." The accident resulted in her niece being permanently scarred. The memory served as a cautionary tale for Taylor to remain "cool under fire." No doubt, Taylor's mother felt forever bound to her niece by their mutual concern for each other and their shared experience of danger. Similarly, Taylor and his soldiers felt bound by their mutual concern for each other and their shared experience of danger.

The third memory was a reminder of the strength and resilience of Taylor's aspirational spirit. This quality was aptly described in a line from a Robert Browning poem, "Ah, but a man's reach should exceed his grasp, Or what's a heaven for?" How could Taylor be afraid of any danger when he recalled himself as someone with limitless energy who fearlessly swam across an icy river? His fear of danger was transformed into a resolve to defy expectations and overcome all obstacles. Perhaps the third memory struck a counterbalancing or redemptive theme, that is: "I would not be the daring and courageous person I am today, if I had not lived through the trials and tribulations of a frontier life. Now, I am bold because during my childhood I knew what it was like to be vulnerable and surrounded by the threat of danger."

The first two memories chronicled the hardships and feelings of anxiety that faced people living on the frontier. People like Taylor's mother and cousin carried physical and emotional scars that resulted from tragic incidents. These negative events helped to shape Taylor's defensive orientation—that is, a tendency to expect and carefully prepare for dangerous situations and be ready to initiate the necessary adjustments. A defensive perspective found tangible form when Taylor anticipated and responded to the dangers of the battlefield—and as President—in his determination to defend the country against the toxic expansion of slavery and the potential Civil War.

The third memory radiated optimism and confidence in Taylor's ability to overcome obstacles. This shaped Taylor's tendency to be selfless and magnanimous. This found tangible form in Taylor's compassion and concern for his troops, the Native Americans, and for the very enemies he fought on the battlefield. He was the fearless and imperturbable warrior who would never quit. In part, Taylor's success in the military, and his success in being elected President, came from reconciling the differences between his offensive and defensive tendencies. It was incumbent upon Taylor to select one or the other perspective: evaluate the risks and benefits, make a decision and take chances.

Taylor's last reported words were:

> *I am about to die—I expect the summons soon—I have endeavored to discharge all my official duties faithfully. I regret nothing, but am sorry that I am about to leave my friends.*

An image of Taylor riding his trusted horse "Old Whitey" reflected a public perception of him—and his perception of himself—as a tireless warhorse with a lifetime of military experience who was not afraid to be at the center of the action. The image of a "Rough and Ready" frontier man, riding on horseback to save a nation, appealed to ordinary voters eager to have someone, similar to themselves, to champion their preferred causes. Taylor may have felt out of place among political insiders and with the social elites. In part, his last words may have been referring to a part of him that wished to be back at home in Kentucky, with his friends—and with his memories of swimming, fishing, hunting and "roaming through forests and boundless prairies."

Perhaps the last word on Zachary Taylor was spoken by Abraham Lincoln: He praised Taylor for his

> *Unostentatious, self-sacrificing, long-enduring devotion to duty. He indulged in no recreations, he visited no public places seeking applause; but quietly, as the earth in its orbit, he was always at his post. Along our whole Indian frontier, through summer and winter, in sunshine and storm, like a sleepless sentinel, he has watched while we have slept for forty long years. How well might the good dying hero say at last, "I have done my duty, I am ready to go."*

Bibliography

Bauer, Jack. Zachary Taylor: Soldier, Planter, Statesman of the Old Southwest. Louisiana State University Press, 1985.
> *Objective and comprehensive appraisal of Zachary Taylor's life.*

Eisenhower, John. Zachary Taylor. New York: Times Books, 2008.

Degregorio, William. The Complete Book of U.S. Presidents. Random House, 1984.

Doak, Robin. Profiles of the Presidents: Zachary Taylor. Compass Point Books, 2003.
> *A brief examination of Zachary Taylor specifically suited for a young adult population.*

Hamilton, Holman. Zachary Taylor: Soldier of the Republic. Bobs – Merrill Company, 1941.

Hamilton, Holman. Zachary Taylor: Soldier in the White House. Bobby- Merrill, 1951.

Lincoln, Abraham. The Life and Public Service of General Zachary Taylor: Eulogy. July 25, 1850.

Montgomery, Henry. The Life of Major General Zachary Taylor. Page 42/3930 – E Book.

Smith, Albert. The Presidencies of Zachary Taylor and Millard Fillmore. University Press of Kansas, 1988.

Franklin Pierce

President of the United States
1853-1857

Memory One: "Listening to Father"

At the commencement of the war of 1812, Franklin Pierce was a few months under eight years of age. The old general, his father, sent two of his sons into the army; and as his eldest daughter was soon afterwards married to Major McNeil, there were few families that had so large a personal stake in the war as that of General Benjamin Pierce ...The general not only took a prominent part in all public meetings, but was ever ready for the informal discussion of political affairs at all places of casual resort ... Franklin Pierce was a frequent auditor of these controversies.
> —*The Life of Franklin Pierce* by Nathaniel Hawthorne;
> e-book: Loc 287 of 1287

The renowned author Nathaniel Hawthorne, Franklin Pierce's college roommate and lifelong best friend, wrote a campaign biography of the president's life. Franklin described his memories of the political discussions that he had overheard as a youngster to his family and friends such as Hawthorne, who wrote,

> *At Franklin Pierce's birth, and for many years subsequent, his father was the most active and public-spirited man within his sphere; a most decided Democrat and supporter of Jefferson and Madison ... Patriotism, such as it had been in the revolutionary days was taught him by his father, as early as his mother taught him religion.*

Franklin's father had been a General in the Revolutionary War and had fought at Ticonderoga, Valley Forge, Bunker Hill and Saratoga. George Washington identified him as one of his most valuable officers. After the war, the elder Pierce entered politics and served two terms as Governor of New Hampshire. Franklin's mother, a native of New Hampshire, had a high-spirited, unconstrained personality but was also prone to depression and alcoholism. One story in a biography by Peter Wallner described his mother attending church wearing a short gown that showed her ankles encircled with red ribbons, causing considerable gossip among the parishioners!

Franklin was the sixth of eight children born to Benjamin and Anna Pierce. He was born on November 23, 1804, at the family's log cabin in Hillsborough, New Hampshire. Shortly after his birth, the Pierces moved into a more spacious frame house that Franklin's father built. The house also served as an inn and tavern. Franklin listened to news of the outside world from the travelers, drinkers and guests. From his father, Franklin listened to heroic tales of the Revolutionary War. As a result, he had a reverence for the military and hoped some day to become a soldier and command troops in battle like his father.

The memory was a reminder that Franklin was expected to follow a code of conduct and stewardship that came with the distinction of being the son of a Brigadier General of the Revolutionary War. Recalling this helped Franklin to define and shape his identity—to determine who he was and who he wanted to be—and conferred a special meaning on his future goals and achievements. The memory depicted the origin of Franklin's fervent patriotism and reflected his desire to single himself out as worthy of becoming a leader in the United States military.

Inspired by the memory, Pierce served in the military and fought for his country in a position of leadership. He served in the Mexican War from 1846 to 1848, during which he was promoted to Brigadier General leading 2,500 men into the swampland of Vera Cruz. He was injured twice but was able to take part in the occupation of the Mexican Capital in 1847. According to biographer Roy Nichols, "While glory had not perched upon his standard he had done his duty. He had shown himself the old General's son."

In part, Pierce modeled himself after the Jeffersonian principles of limited Government and states' rights that his father actively promoted at the inn. As a United States Congressman from New

Hampshire (1833–1837) he opposed the federally controlled Bank of the United States and supported a gag rule that prevented the federal government from intervening on behalf of abolishing slavery. In fact, Pierce denounced Abolitionists as "reckless fanatics." He served as a congressman under President Andrew Jackson, "Old Hickory," and acquired the nickname "Young Hickory" because of his devotion to Jacksonian and Jeffersonian principles such as limiting the federal government's powers.

Although Pierce was a loyal and principled Democrat, it can be argued that politically his fatal flaw was a too-strict adherence to the Jeffersonian and Jacksonian principles on which he was raised. Even Pierce's lifetime best friend and the author of his flattering campaign biography, Nathaniel Hawthorne observed, "It would ruin this noble character, though one of limited scope, for him to admit any ideas that were not entertained by the Fathers of the Constitution and the Republic."

Although Pierce was not a slave owner, he believed that the principle of states' rights transcended the rights of African-Americans to be free from slavery. As he stated in his Inaugural Address:

> *I believe that involuntary servitude, as it exists in different States of this Confederacy, is recognized by the Constitution. I believe that it stands like any other admitted right, and that the States where it exists are entitled to efficient remedies to enforce the constitutional provisions ... I fervently hope that the question is at rest, and that no sectional or ambitious or fanatical excitement may again threaten the durability of our institutions or obscure the light of our prosperity.*

Pierce may have viewed himself as a principled and patriotic figure who was devoted to constitutional principles. However, as President, to many citizens of the sharply divided electorate, he was not seen as principled. This was particularly the case when Pierce described the Fugitive Slave Law as inhumane but compelled the authorities to enforce it. Although Pierce's father might have applauded his son's stance on states' rights and limiting federal power, his son's actions left both Northerners and Southerners feeling that he was favoring the other side.

President Pierce supported the Kansas-Nebraska Act of 1854 which negated the terms of the Missouri Compromise of 1820 that prohibited expansion of slavery into the Louisiana territory. Pierce supported the notion of "Popular Sovereignty" in which the citizens of Kansas and Nebraska had the right to vote for slavery if they wanted it. The Act initiated a violent struggle between pro-slavery settlers and settlers who wanted the Kansas territory to be free. As violence and bloodshed became more frequent throughout "Bleeding Kansas," Pierce was viewed by Northerners as a Southern sympathizer, and by Southerners as an ineffective advocate for their cause. As a result, support for Pierce plummeted and he became the only President not to be nominated by his own party for a second term. Accordingly, during the 1856 Democratic convention, one slogan that was used by Pierce's own party was: "Anybody but Pierce."

A memory inspiring Pierce to follow in his father's footsteps provided an overall framework into which he could fit his political, social, economic and personal beliefs—beliefs on such issues as leadership, slavery, loyalty and state sovereignty. Professional challenges in Pierce's life were seen as an opportunity to renew and strengthen the principles that were passed on to him by his father at the inn. Hearing his father tell exciting tales about the Revolutionary War encouraged Pierce to become a military leader and foreshadowed how he would later become a Brigadier General during the Mexican War. Moreover, at the age of twelve, two of Pierce's older brothers and his half-sister's husband fought in the War of 1812. Young Pierce also listened to stories of their heroism at the inn, which further reinforced his desire to follow the family tradition of military involvement.

Memory Two: "Homesick"

In analyzing this memory we discover an apparent contradiction in Franklin's character. His support and advocacy for states' rights has already been noted, including the laws protecting and enforcing slavery, although not a slave owner himself. Yet, as this memory will reveal, he also manifested a strongly compassionate nature toward those he viewed as vulnerable or needy, even to the detriment of his own comfort and safety.

When Franklin Pierce was twelve, he attended Hancock Academy, a private school a few miles from his home. Franklin grew homesick. One day he decided to go home. He slipped away from the school early on a Sunday morning and trudged homeward. He arrived at the big white house when everyone was at church and waited fearfully for his father to come home. The general looked at his son and said nothing. They went into Sunday dinner and talked of family things. It was just like always, and young Franklin was content.

But after dinner, the general had the carriage hitched up to his favorite horse. He beckoned to a quailing Franklin, who suddenly realized that he was being sent back to school. What is more, he was taught a lesson. The general took Franklin just halfway, then turned him out of the carriage and told him to walk the rest of the way back to the Academy. It was a lesson in obedience which Franklin recalled in later life.

—*Franklin Pierce*; by Edwin P. Hoyt, page19.

The memory allows us to witness firsthand what was going on in Pierce's mind at the age of twelve. Perhaps one reason he admired his father was that he turned a potentially embarrassing and negative experience into a teachable moment. Effective discipline can be learned from a book or lecture, but somehow its importance is heightened by recalling a moment from the past when it was actually experienced. Perhaps a memory of his father's gentle guidance was the beginning of Pierce's journey as a compassionate and caring person. In this context, the memory encouraged him to model after his father's example of supporting others who were vulnerable—notwithstanding his view that states' rights superseded the inhumanity of slavery.

Nathaniel Hawthorne wrote that while attending Hancock Academy, Pierce was known for his "cordial sympathy." In one case,

> *One of his classmates, being older than most of his companions,
> and less advanced in his studies, found it difficult to keep up
> with the class ... while the other boys were at play, Franklin
> spent the noon recess, for many weeks together, in aiding him
> in his lesson. These attributes have remained with him through
> life.*

Hawthorne also commented on Pierce's compassionate actions as a
General during the Mexican War:

> *His tenderness of heart, his sympathy, his brotherly or paternal
> care for his men, had been displayed in a hundred instances,
> and had gained him the enthusiastic affection of all who served
> under his command—While encamped before Vera Cruz, he
> gave up his own tent to a sick comrade, and went himself to
> lodge in the pestilential city. And, in the hospitals of Mexico, he
> went among the diseased and wounded soldiers, cheering them
> with his voice and the magic of his kindness, inquiring into
> their wants, and relieving them to the utmost of his pecuniary
> means.*

Another example of Pierce demonstrating compassion for others
involved his wife, Jane Appleton Pierce, with whom he took a
protective and nurturing role. Jane Appleton was the daughter of the
former President of Bowdoin College from which Pierce graduated.
Biographer Roy Nichols described Jane as "shy, retiring, frail and
tubercular." She was also religious, hated politics as well as public
life, and was distressed by her husband's excessive drinking. In
Nichols' estimation, "Her delicate health and retiring disposition
made her an appealing object for his solicitude."

Perhaps Pierce's kindness and compassion toward the vulnerable
was prompted by the memory of his own mother's labile mentality.
When a close friend asked Pierce why he married Jane, Pierce
replied, "I could take better care of her than anyone else."
Accordingly, Pierce may have unconsciously selected an emotionally
and physically needy partner in order to help her, prove his own
strength and conceal his own feelings of vulnerability. He would

become disillusioned and depressed when his efforts proved to be unsuccessful.

Pierce and his wife lost all three of their children. The first child died within days of his birth and the second died of typhus at the age of four. The last child, eleven-year-old Benjamin, was killed in a tragic train crash a few months before Pierce took office. A jolt caused the train car in which the family was riding to derail into a field below. Benjamin was caught in the wreckage and killed before his parents' eyes. Jane was inconsolable after the accident and never fully recovered from it. She opposed his decision to run for president; and when her son died in the accident, she interpreted it as an act of God that was designed to free up his time and remove any distractions from his presidential responsibilities.

Throughout his presidency, Pierce would be emotionally distracted by his son's death—blaming himself for what happened and for his wife's ill-health. His son's tragic death worked itself into his inaugural address: "It is a relief to feel that no heart but my own can know the personal regret and bitter sorrow over which I have been born to a position so suitable for others rather than desirable for myself." For two years after Benjamin's death his wife remained in the upstairs living quarters of the White House, spending her days writing cathartic letters to her dead son. People began to call her "the Shadow of the White House." But President Pierce held it together, leading the nation for four years when it would have been easier to "run away" as he did in the memory. Perhaps, an image of his father's gentle guidance helped him to cope and process the losses he sustained with each one of his children as well as with his wife's intense grief.

The memory suggested that Pierce was dependent on his parents' love and acceptance of him and served as an admonition to use better self-control lest he lose his father's approval. The loss of parental approval played itself out with Franklin's mother as well. A former playmate recalled a time when Pierce fell into the river getting his clothes all wet. He feared disapproval and possible punishment by his mother; so he convinced his friend's mother to dry and iron his clothes before he returned home. His exceptional personal charm was revealed by the playmate's remark, "My mother said you was so agreeable in conversation that day she almost fell in love with you."

Perhaps Pierce was so dependent on his family's support and guidance that he felt anxious and insecure when others failed to appreciate his efforts. In part, Pierce may have run away from the Hancock Academy because he was concerned that he would be unable to fulfill the school's standards or expectations; or that if he remained at the school he would be unable to prove himself worthy of his family's high expectations. The memory may have helped Pierce to release and process some of the pressure that others placed upon him or that he placed upon himself.

When Pierce left the Presidency in 1857, the United States was more disordered then when he assumed office four years earlier. Unable to please either his party or the electorate, the Democrats passed over Pierce and nominated James Buchanan, who had served as a minister to England during Pierce's administration. Asked what a president should do after leaving office, Pierce remarked, "There's nothing left ... but to get drunk!"

Pierce's memory of his father's kindness and compassion toward him may have fostered his own compassion for others in need. The memory foreshadowed Franklin's concern of whether he would ever become truly independent of his family. At the age of twelve, Franklin's view of himself was evolving. Would he be independent and self-assured, like his father? Or would he be prone to depression and alcoholism, dependent on others, as was his mother?

Memory Three: "The Melon Patch"

Franklin led a gang of boys on a summer night raid on a neighbor's melon patch. The boys were caught red-handed, but Pierce, the ringleader, took full responsibility for the crime. "I did it, Sir, and I'm ready to take the consequences—the others were my guests, and on me rests the responsibility for the whole affair."
    —Franklin Pierce: New Hampshire's Favorite Son, P. Wallner, p. 11.

If we remember past events that make us feel the most anxious, then this memory has its roots in Pierce's belief that things don't always go as planned. When young Pierce said, "on me rests the responsibility for the whole affair" he was hoping that his urge to be a rule-breaker could be offset by a strong sense of social justice.

The memory offers numerous insights into Pierce's character. He was an inveterate schemer, rule-breaker, leader of his peers, and a charming child who could win over adults. The appeal that so many people admired in later life was on display at an early age. Coupled with Pierce's likability was a set of ethical principles such as the honesty he displayed in the memory—regardless of what the consequences might be. As a result, Pierce encompassed both the capacity for being principled and the capacity for being mischievous.

Pierce wanted to emulate both the leadership characteristics of his renowned father and the demonstrative affection of his mother. According to biographer Roy Nichols, Pierce's mother was

> *… vivacious, fond of show and of an effervescing, mercurial temperament which occasionally sought refuge in alcoholic stimulant—between his father's strictness and his mother's easy-going ways there was sure to be a chance for the quick-witted to escape many of the consequences of boyish disobedience.*

Pierce himself wrote of his mother,

> *She was the most affectionate and tender mother, strong in many points and weak in some but always weak on the side of kindness and deep affection—when others chided and reproached she never failed to interpose excuses and justification.*

Pierce operated politically like his principled father and personally like his compassionate mother. On one hand, like his father, he zealously supported Jeffersonian and Jacksonian principles. On the other hand, like his mother, he was easy-going and amiable. Pierce struggled to find the right balance between these competing tendencies—pleasing others while following his convictions and principles.

One example of how Pierce tried to blend the two tendencies happened during his senior year at Bowdoin College. During the winter vacation, Pierce traveled to a friend's home to teach in the local school district. A twelve-year-old student in Pierce's class, and later a Republican congressman wrote:

> *It was true that two or three of the older boys thought they would try the mettle of the young New Hampshire collegian, but it only took one or two old-fashioned floggings to cure them of all such delusive ideas. The father of one student took offense to his son's punishment and confronted Pierce. Pierce met him with one of his blandest smiles, shook him heartily by the hand, invited him to the school room, gave him his own chair, told him how pleased he was to see him, and so mesmerized him with special attention and kind words that the old fellow forgot what he was there for, and very soon quietly retired and ever after was one of Pierce's best friends.*

Pierce's actions in the narrative reflected both his wish to be a dominating leader and to offset an angry parent by being charming. In other words, did he want to be more like his father and assume the role of a strict but caring disciplinarian? Or, did he want to be more like his mother and assume the role of a charmer who handled conflict in a beguiling manner? Recalling this event may have made it easier for Pierce to consider these opposing tendencies within himself. Moreover, it provided him with an opportunity to select from two different parenting styles his own preferred version of himself.

As a sixteen-year-old student at Bowdoin College, Pierce continued to defy the rules in a manner that the memory presaged. For example, some of the rules at Bowdoin were as follows:

> *No student shall eat or drink in any tavern unless in company with his parent or guardian, nor attend any theatrical entertainment or any idle show in Brunswick, nor play at cards, billiards, or any game of hazard, nor go shooting or fishing. No student shall be*

concerned in loud and disorderly singing in College, in shouting or clapping hands. Students must be in their rooms Saturday and Sunday evenings and abstain from diversions of every kind. They who profane the Sabbath by necessary business, visiting or receiving visits, or by walking abroad, or by any amusement, or in other ways, may be admonished or suspended.

Encumbered by these overbearing rules, Pierce responded in a playfully rebellious manner, exhibiting the same contrary behavior that was expressed in the memory. For example, in the Bowdoin dormitory, Pierce was known for invading other students' rooms in order to initiate furniture-smashing wrestling matches. Moreover, according to biographer Edwin P. Hoyt, Pierce spent many hours skipping classes, "wandering in the cool, clean Maine woods and then hours in less acceptable pursuits such as visiting an old woman who told fortunes with a pack of tattered cards and frequenting the forbidden taverns."

In part, Pierce's oppositional behavior was designed to renounce the inflexible rules and expectations that he perceived Bowdoin College imposed on him. Similarly, his actions in the memory of the melon patch raid may have been designed to free himself from some of the moral absolutes on which he was raised by his strict father and religious mother.

Both before and during his political career, Pierce exhibited a maverick streak that was expressed in the memory. For example, Pierce was a loyal Democrat, but he was known to deviate from the party line when he felt their proposals were inconsistent with the principles of limited federal power and states' rights. Accordingly, as a United States Congressman under President Andrew Jackson, Pierce opposed any action—even if Jackson himself supported it—in which the federal government sponsored legislation to improve the infrastructure of the whole nation, such as waterways and railroads. In this regard, some Democrats argued that Pierce "out-Jacksoned Jackson."

Memory Four: "Turning Point"

Soon after the beginning of his third year at Bowdoin College, the relative standings of the men were announced. Pierce went to scan the list and found that his was the lowest in his class. This was too much for his pride and bitterly he decided never to attend another recitation. This resolution he proceeded to carry out and for several days he moped. Determined to "come back," for three months Pierce rose at four and retired at twelve, devoting unceasing labor to repairing the inroads of idleness.

In this campaign for reconstruction he had the continuous aid of his friend Caldwell whose burning eyes and feverish earnestness considerably influenced him. In order to help in the struggle for discipline, Caldwell turned over to him his duties as chapel monitor. So successful was this campaign, that Pierce never again missed a class or an exercise (with two exceptions) nor went to a class unprepared. By the end of his senior year Pierce had risen from last place to fifth in his class and had the honor of delivering a seven-minute disquisition in Latin on "The Influence of Circumstances on the Intellectual Character."

—Franklin Pierce: Young Hickory of the Granite Hills,
Roy Franklin Nichols, pp. 21-22.

In Nathaniel Hawthorne's campaign biography of Pierce he opined, "The moral of this little story lies in the stern and continued exercise of self-controlling will, which redeemed Pierce from indolence, completely changed the aspect of his character and made this the turning point of his life."

Pierce spent the first two years of college struggling to reconcile his bifurcated perspective of himself. The first perspective was an image of himself as at the bottom of the class and depicted him as being irresponsible, unworthy and shameful. This "down and out" feeling was unsettling to him, yet the discomfort motivated him to survive the last two years of college and to realize his potential along with a sense of hope for the future. The second perspective was an image of himself at the top of his class—finishing fifth and delivering the disquisition in Latin—and depicted him as disciplined, responsible and strong enough to overcome his initial sense of failure.

In the memory, Pierce was asking himself if he was in control of his destiny or if he was fated to be undone by temptation and lack of discipline—perhaps like his mother? Could he will himself to succeed at school or would his life be determined by inherited circumstances beyond his control? Should he live the life of a rule-breaker at Bowdoin or be a dedicated and diligent student? When Pierce "scanned the list" and discovered that he ranked last, he had a moment of epiphany—he was not the kind of son, student or person he wanted to be—and he was determined to reform himself. Instead of hiking in the woods, visiting fortune tellers and drinking in the taverns, Pierce attended all of his classes, became chapel monitor, captain of a military company of students, and chairman of the Athenian Literary Society.

The memory foreshadowed the way in which Pierce would process negative events and laid the groundwork for how he would handle future setbacks. In short, it communicated the following message: "I have high standards and I do not want to be in last place. I am responsible for my actions and I will use this memory of my low ranking to motivate me, to set my expectations high and to be more disciplined than I ever thought possible."

The memory celebrated the birthplace of Pierce's will to succeed and his determination never to surrender to defeat. In effect, he was the "ugly duckling" who felt belittled at the beginning but found respectability at the end. Similarly, in the memory, Pierce was ashamed of his ranking at the beginning, but at the end he felt worthy and equal to his college peers. The memory honored Pierce's struggle to overcome his diminished self-esteem and prepared him to conquer any challenge in his path. This carried forward when, as a young lawyer, Pierce lost his first case. When a friend offered him encouragement, Pierce replied,

> *I do not need that. I will try nine-hundred-and-ninety-nine cases, if clients will continue to trust me, and if I fail just as I have today, I will try the thousandth. I shall live to argue cases*

> *in this courthouse in a manner that will mortify neither myself nor my friends.*

Throughout his life, Pierce would face many dramatic reversals of fortune where one moment he was on top and the next moment he was at the bottom. His leadership abilities, talent for political maneuvering and easy-going manner helped him to achieve many early successes such as being elected to the New Hampshire legislature at age twenty-four, Speaker of the state legislature at age twenty-seven, U.S. Congressman at age twenty-nine, and U.S. Senator at age thirty-three. Yet, his political triumphs were followed by the tragic deaths of all three of his children—the youngest an eleven-year-old who was killed in a railroad accident.

He was invited by President James K. Polk to serve as Attorney General—but declined because his wife resented the alcoholic temptations to which Washingtonian politics exposed him. He achieved the rank of Brigadier General during the Mexican War, yet his critics vilified him for an unimpressive military record. For example, they mocked Pierce for a battlefield incident when his horse reared-up and he fell and passed out, earning the title, "Fainting Frank." Another slight was when the Whigs distributed a book called "The Military Services of Gen. Pierce" which was one-inch high by a half-inch wide; and alluded to his alcoholism by calling him "The hero of many a well-fought bottle."

Pierce had many laudable accomplishments during his administration such as acquiring land from Mexico in the Gadsden Purchase, in what became southern Arizona and New Mexico; initiating the nation's first trade agreement with Japan; advocating for the rights of immigrants; and the first President to appoint a Jewish ambassador. Yet, he was lampooned as a reckless negotiator for demanding that Spain sell Cuba to the United States for one-hundred-twenty million dollars under an implied threat of war. Moreover, he was so unpopular as a result of his support for the Kansas-Nebraska Act that his own Democratic Party failed to nominate him for a second term.

Pierce was praised by Nathaniel Hawthorne for having "many of the chief elements of a great ruler. His talents are administrative, he has a subtle faculty of making affairs roll onward according to his will, and of influencing their course without showing any trace of his action." Yet, he was criticized by Theodore Roosevelt as a "small politician of low capacity and mean surroundings, proud to act as the servile tool of men worse than himself but also stronger and abler. He was ever ready to do any work the slavery leaders set him."

Nevertheless, Pierce defended his administration in a letter to his cabinet at the end of his term:

> *[They] could be proud of the condition of the country during the four years about to close. There were no defalcations [misappropriation of funds] on the part of federal officers and the treasury was free from the touch of fraud or speculation. Foreign affairs had been amicably and advantageously adjusted and peace maintained without component or right or a stain upon the national honor.*

It was only much later in his life that Pierce realized the importance of not measuring himself against the rankings of others or even by his own self-imposed rankings. He could only listen to critical feedback, forgive himself for any possible lapses and move on, just as he tried to redeem himself in the memory when he scanned the class rankings. When Abraham Lincoln was assassinated in 1865, crowds gathered in Concord, New Hampshire, to seek out those homes where there was no visible sign of mourning for the fallen President. When they arrived at ex-president Pierce's home they demanded that he show his loyalty to Lincoln and the Union by displaying the United States flag. Pierce refused to be intimidated, remarking to the crowd:

> *It is not necessary for me to show my devotion for the Stars and Stripes by any special exhibitions. If the period which I have served our state and country in various situations, commencing more than 35 years ago, has left in doubt about the question of my devotion to the flag, the Constitution and*

the Union, it is too late now to rescue it with any such exhibition.

Even if his fellow New Hampshire citizens considered him disrespectful—if not treasonous—for not honoring Lincoln's legacy in the manner they wanted to see, Pierce chose to defend his lifetime of service to his country. The crowd listened to Pierce's heartfelt and straightforward words and dispersed.

For some time before he became President, Pierce abstained from alcohol, joined the Temperance movement, and led a successful drive to outlaw alcohol in Concorde, New Hampshire. After his presidency he struggled with grief, depression and relapsed to excessive drinking. Shunned and virtually forgotten, Pierce died in 1869 from cirrhosis of the liver. His most enduring legacy may be that his name consistently appears near the bottom of all the presidential rankings, along with James Buchanan and Andrew Johnson—a dubious distinction first foreshadowed in the memory.

Summary

In the first memory, Pierce overheard his father tell stories at the family inn about his service in the Revolutionary War and that of his brothers in the War of 1812. He may have experienced a sense of inadequacy in comparison to his family's achievements. It was not easy to carry on the family heritage and live up to their high standards of political and military leadership. Nevertheless, the memory motivated Pierce to emulate his family's accomplishments and become a success in the military and in politics. Pierce's commitment to the ideals communicated to him by his father in the memory, and his wish to emulate those accomplishments, represent a valuable reminder of why an early memory matters.

In the second memory Pierce runs away from school in order to return to the safety and comfort of his home. The memory expressed Pierce's internal struggle between the desire to be taken care of and the wish for independence. In addition, the memory presaged

Pierce's empathic manner, modeled after his father's caring and supportive reaction.

In the third memory Pierce led a gang of boys on a summer-night raid at a neighbor's melon patch. When the gang was caught, the impulse to protect them seemed to be instinctive and Pierce admitted responsibility for the caper. Pierce learned from the memory to think of himself as both a rule-breaker and a trustworthy friend. Moreover, the memory helped him to step back and thoughtfully identify constructive strategies to channel his ethical principles and talent for leadership. His history of opposing the established order had its roots in the melon patch, continued at Bowdoin College and lasted throughout his political career.

In the last memory Pierce learns that success and failure are two sides of the same coin. The memory provided him with a way to understand himself amidst the constant ups-and-downs in his life and motivated him to fight his way back from the bottom by being disciplined and determined. Would he be a disciplined winner and live up to his family's expectations of him, or would he be a loser, a likable dunce who was more interested in having fun than he was in studying?

Even if Pierce consistently appears near the bottom of presidential rankings, he should be viewed as more than a one-dimensional individual, a southern sympathizer from the north who supported the Kansas-Nebraska Act because he considered the rights of African-Americans secondary to states' rights. Together the four memories indicate that as a lawyer, Congressman, Senator, Brigadier General and President, Pierce was a complex and nuanced man who equated his own principles and values with the best interests of the United States. As President of a nation that was vexed by internal conflict, he tried to promote his principles and values to the best of his ability, despite his personal problems and individual failings.

Bibliography

Gara, Larry. The Presidency of Franklin Pierce. Lawrence: University Press of Kansas, 1991.

Hawthorne, Nathaniel. The Life of Franklin Pierce. Boston; Ticknor, Reed, and Fields, 1852.

Hawthorne, Nathaniel. The Life of Franklin Pierce. E Book: Loc 287 of 1287.

Holt, Michael. Franklin Pierce. The American Presidents Series: N.Y. Times Books, 2010.

Hoyt, Edwin. Franklin Pierce. New York, Abelard- Schuman, 1972.

Nichols, Roy Franklin. Franklin Pierce; Young Hickory of the Granite Hills. Philadelphia; University of Pennsylvania Press, 1931, completely revised edition 1958.
> *This book provides thorough and detailed information about Pierce's life as well as his character.*

Wallner, Peter A. Franklin Pierce: Martyr for the Union. Concorde, N.H.:Plaidswede, 2007.

Wallner, Peter A. Franklin Pierce: New Hampshire's Favorite Son, Concorde, N.H.: Plaidswede, 2004.

Andrew Johnson

President of the United States
1865-1869

Memory One: "Poor White Trash"

Andrew could hardly miss feeling the striking contrast between himself and the elite. Unlike the children of the rich, he never had a day's schooling in his life; his mother was too poor to afford it, and there were no public schools in Raleigh. And the aristocrats' contempt was scarcely hidden. When Andrew and his cousins once ran across the path between the house of John Devereaux and that of his son, Devereaux sent his coachman to whip the boys back to their shanty— they were running naked, according to Devereaux's granddaughter. Whatever the truth of this particular incident, the whip was habitually used on those that Devereaux called "poor white trash."
—Andrew Johnson: A Biography by Hans L. Trefousse p.21.

Andrew Johnson was born in 1808 in a log cabin in Raleigh, North Carolina. At the age of three, his father, Jacob Johnson, died of an apparent heart attack shortly after rescuing three drowning men. Johnson's father had been a porter and his mother, Mary, worked as a washerwoman and became the sole support of the penniless family. Both parents were illiterate. Elizabeth, Andrew's older sister and the second child, died during childhood. Shortly after the death of Andrew's father, his mother married again, this time to another impoverished man named Turner Doughtry. To make ends meet, Andrew's mother apprenticed her oldest son, William to a tailor. At the age of fourteen Andrew was also apprenticed to another tailor and the contract called for him to remain "a 'bound boy' till he arrived at lawful age to earn the trade of a Tailor (twenty-one)."

A boyhood friend of Johnson depicted the brutal realities Andrew faced growing up poor at the beginning of the nineteenth century:

"Some people can boast of a grand start; I reckon he started underground."

The memory represented Johnson's perceived truth about the social divide between the rich and poor during his childhood. Moreover, the memory represented a divide between Johnson's feelings of social and economic powerlessness and his deep-seated anger and resentment for "stuck-up aristocrats." In the memory, Mr. Devereaux and the coachman were portrayed as ruthless, people who were capable of physically and emotionally damaging an impoverished child who was born on the "wrong side of the tracks."

A memory about beginning his life in poverty and facing a daunting challenge to his self-worth functioned as a catalyst for Johnson to initiate bold and aggressive actions to overcome his lowly status, restore a sense of control over his fate and gain respect from those who looked down on him. According to biographer Lately Thomas, "Throughout his whole life, when faced by any unjust assumption of superiority or power, both his instinct and his will forbade him to knuckle under."

Full of fury that he was considered "poor white trash" and driven by the fear of insignificance that the memory implied, Johnson tended to verbally lash out at others. A reporter remarked that in his political speeches, Johnson "cut and slashed right and left, tore big wounds and left something behind to fester and remember." Johnson treated his adversaries as contemptuously as he was treated by Mr. Devereux and the coachman. The memory provides an explanation for Johnson's bitterness—a bitterness that was captured in a statement made by one of his political adversaries: "If Johnson were a snake, he would hide himself in the grass by the heels of the children of rich people."

The image of a child running naked across a path was a metaphor that explained Johnson's identification with the economically and socially disenfranchised; an identification that more wealthy and better educated politicians lacked. There is something ironic and touching in the memory of an impoverished child who later became an apprenticed tailor, struggling to find his place in an unfair world without the necessary resources (clothes) to be successful. The memory linked the origins of Johnson's impoverished beginnings to a theme that would define his political identity—that he hated the social and economic plight of the poor and he was committed to being their champion, someone who would protect them from the uncaring aristocrats.

In part, Johnson's rise to the presidency can be attributed to a brassy, hard-hitting and blunt style that showed contempt for his political opposition. Sometimes, Johnson's contemptuous comments for others represented a desire to dominate or control them. In other cases, his contemptuousness represented an unforgiving vindictiveness for his so-called "betters" —the first of whom was Mr. Devereaux. In either case, as a politician, Johnson wanted to correct the wrongs that the poor suffered at the hands of the southern planter class, injustices that he painfully experienced as a child.

In 1853, at the start of his first term as Governor of Tennessee, Johnson demonstrated his identification with the common man by walking rather than riding in a carriage to his own inauguration. Governor Johnson promoted public schools and public libraries in order to improve conditions for the common man. He asked the people of Tennessee, "Whose hands built your Capitol? Whose toil, whose labor built your railroads and your ships? I say let the mechanic and the laborer make our laws, rather than the idle and vicious aristocrat." Johnson's lack of pretension, common touch and refusal to put on airs was rooted in the humbling memory.

Johnson never got over his childhood deprivations and the experience of being looked down upon by—as he called them—"the illegitimate, swaggering, scrub aristocracy." For example, while serving as a United States Congressman in 1845, he wrote to a friend in Greeneville, Tennessee, the state to which he had moved at the age of eighteen:

> *I never want to own another foot of dirt in the dam [sic] town while I live—If I should happen to die among the dam spirits that infest Greeneville, I would bequeath the last dollar to some negro to pay to take my dirty, stinky carcass after death, out on some*

mountain peak and there leave it to be devoured by the vultures and wolves, or that it might pass off in smoke and ride upon the wind in triumph over the god-forsaken and Hell-deserving, money-loving, hypocritical, back- biting, Sunday-praying, scoundrels of the town of Greeneville.

During the time period in which the memory took place, Johnson was not at the bottom of the social ladder—African-Americans were. As pointed out by biographer Hans L. Trefousse:

After all, he was white, a fact that gave him a standing immeasurably higher than that of Raleigh's numerous blacks. Although he freely played with mulatto children, he certainly could not escape the ingrained racism so prevalent in Southern society. Poor whites looked down on blacks, slave and free. Moreover, they disliked non-whites—fears of social and economic competition could hardly have occasioned friendly feelings.

As a politician, Johnson's outlook on Reconstruction and racial equality were shaped by his fear that African-Americans posed a significant threat to poor whites, such as himself in the memory. As Johnson once explained it, if a certain congressional bill passed, "It would place every splay-footed, bandy-shanked, hump-backed, thick-lipped, flat-nosed, wooly-headed, ebony colored Negro in the country upon an equality with the poor white man." Moreover, when he became President, Johnson even told a delegation of blacks that the aristocracy and their slaves were involved in a conspiracy to oppress poor white people by preventing them from rising to take their rightful place in the economy. Johnson's feelings included both contempt for the wealthy aristocrats at the top and for African-Americans at the bottom of the socioeconomic ladder.

Perhaps Johnson appreciated his opportunity to rise to the top only inasmuch as African-Americans were deprived of such opportunities. Johnson seemed to be caught in a self-perpetuating belief system; that is, he looked down on African-Americans just as the "scrub-aristocracy" looked down on him. He felt superior to those who enhanced his sense of power and distracted him from his own feelings of inferiority. Johnson may have felt threatened that if

African-Americans overcame social and economic barriers, it would somehow diminish his own rags-to-riches story. Perhaps African-Americans who succeeded would have received even more acclaim than he did, given that they actually rose from the absolute bottom of the social ladder.

During his Presidency, Johnson believed that Reconstruction was inimical to economic stability and would undermine well-established social norms. He believed that the government had not given poor whites special treatment, so poor African-Americans should not receive special treatment during Reconstruction. When Southern states passed Black Codes that limited the rights of African-Americans—such as the right to vote and where they could live, work and travel—Johnson maintained that the states had the authority to implement such laws and that the federal government could not supersede their authority.

During Reconstruction, Johnson remarked, "This is a country for white men, and by God, as long as I am president, it shall be a government for white men." Johnson did not support the Freedmen's Bureau (1865), which was designed "to devise a new social order between freed men (former slaves) and former masters." In addition, Johnson vetoed a Civil Rights Act that was subsequently overturned by Congress—the first time a presidential veto of major legislation was overturned.

In the memory, young Andrew ran naked across the path; and throughout his life all he could do was to keep running, stopping only when necessary and then resuming at a quick pace until he reached the finish line. He ran through a stratified class system that he felt was rigged in favor of the rich. He believed he had been exposed to an unfair and degrading childhood and he carried this perception forward long after the original disturbing events occurred. His contentious personality masked a reservoir of rage and resentment. Johnson never forgot the humiliation he experienced in the memory and those feelings influenced both the course of Reconstruction and the trajectory of race relations in America into the 20th century.

Memory Two: "Reading aloud"

In Selby's tailor shop, Johnson toiled from early morning to evening, sitting cross-legged on the tailor's bench, bending over a hot "goose" [a heavy iron] pressing, stitching, patching, cutting, binding, raveling— with no letup except for meals. Unlike the other boys, however, he wanted to learn. He felt that he must master the ability to read ... there was one person of education, Dr. William G. Hill, who devoted his leisure to reading aloud in Selby's shop. His favorite book was a collection of the orations of Charles James Fox, William Pitt and Edmund Burke and other British statesmen called The American Speaker... *Somehow Andrew managed to teach himself to read simple words ... a feat requiring superior determination. One day, after Hill had read a stirring passage from his* Speaker, *Andy begged to borrow the book. The doctor replied that if Andy could show that he could read, the book would be his to keep. Andrew thereupon did demonstrate that he could puzzle out words, and received the gift. It was his first book.*

—*The First President Johnson*, by Lately Thomas, page 13.

About the book Johnson later said:

There was one book in particular that I believed formed a turning point in my life; that is, it caused my thoughts to take a channel which they might not and probably would not have otherwise taken—When I was learning my trade at Raleigh, North Carolina, a gentleman used to come into the shop and read aloud, and seeing that we tailors enjoyed it so much, he used frequently to come, and finally gave me the book, which was the first property I ever owned. How many times I have read the book I am unable to say, but I am satisfied it caused my life to take a different turn from what it otherwise would."

—Dave Odegard: *The Favorite Books Of All 44 Presidents Of The United States.*

This memory infused Johnson with the love of reading, at which point he would emulate the successes of the esteemed statesmen cited in the book. The uplifting memory of Dr. Hill reading *The*

American Speaker to him, and then giving him the book, offered Johnson a sense of comfort when he felt anxious, demoralized or hopeless. Biographer Lately Thomas reported that during Johnson's impeachment proceedings:

> *Johnson seldom discussed the trial any more, but often talked about his early youth. One day he brought out a battered copy of The American Speaker, and asked Moore (his secretary) to read the passages from Chatham's speeches from it. He had learned to read from a copy of that book, the President said; it had been given to him by William Hill. How ardently I wished I could read like Bill Hill!*

Johnson found comfort in having his secretary read to him the same way an uneducated but aspirational child found comfort in Dr. Hill reading to him at the tailor shop. The memory stood out in opposition to the negative consequences he imagined would unfold as a result of the impeachment proceedings. The memory reflected Johnson in his best light, an ordinary boy with extraordinary ambition and tenacity. According to historian John Robert Irelan,

> The American Speaker *in the hands of this unknown reader put him on the way to the Presidency. The taste for reading and desire for self-improvement started at this time never left him; and the determination, formed doubtlessly in the shop at Raleigh, "to be something" he never abandoned.*

The American Speaker also included advice on public speaking and helped to shape Johnson's subsequent interest in debating and oratory. For example, in 1828, Johnson owned a small but thriving tailor shop in Greeneville, Tennessee. The tailor who never attended a day of school would walk four miles to Greeneville College to take part in the local debating society. In 1843, when Johnson went to Washington, D.C. as a Democratic congressman from Tennessee, he had established a reputation for delivering impassioned, crowd-pleasing speeches.

One oratorical strategy in the book encouraged the reader to "Learn to speak slow, all other graces Will follow in their places."

Apparently, Johnson followed this oratorical tip because Oliver Temple, the Whig candidate whom Johnson defeated in the 1847 House race, remarked:

> *His delivery, if not elegant, was at least easy, natural, and pleasing. His flow of language was wonderful considering he was uneducated and inexperienced as a speaker. Put him against an inferior and he would triumph; put him against a superior and he would acquit himself with credit. I'm not sure he ever met his match.*

In1853, when Johnson campaigned for the Governorship of Tennessee, against a man known as the "Eagle Orator," his opponent admonished his supporters not to underestimate the tailor-politician, remarking, "I have never met so powerful a speaker as Andrew Johnson."

The foreman at Mr. Selby's tailor shop, James Litchford, remembered young Andrew as "a wild harum-scarum boy with no unhonorable traits." The memory enabled Johnson to entertain the possibility that one day even a "harum-scarum" boy could obtain social, occupational and financial respectability. He could do this if he practiced his oratorical style and modeled himself after the speech habits of the individuals cited in the book; and from Dr. Hill and other assigned readers he listened to as he cut cloth and sewed at the tailor shop. Furthermore, the memory enabled Johnson to identify with exemplary father-figures from the book who served as stand-ins for his own father who died when he was three years old.

Inspired by the memory, Johnson set his expectations high. He sought recognition and acclaim by developing a successful tailoring business in his hometown of Greeneville, Tennessee; and he prospered financially in real estate deals, rising steadily through every level of government. He served as a town alderman (1828), Mayor (1835), state Senator (1841), U.S. Congressman (1842), Governor (1853), U.S. Senator (1857), Brigadier General (1862), Vice President (1864), President (1865), and the only former President to subsequently serve as a U.S. Senator (1875).

As President, Johnson pressed for economy in government and dedicated himself to making sure that underprivileged and under-educated citizens had a chance to learn and succeed. In this vein, Johnson advanced the Homestead Act, which issued land to needy settlers. Furthermore, he vetoed a proposal to sell government land to a New York mining company, remarking: "The public domain is a national trust—not to be bestowed as a special privilege upon a favorite class." In 1867, Johnson's Secretary of State, William Seward, completed a land deal with Russia in which the United States purchased Alaska for over seven million dollars. The same person who recalled that a single book was "the first property I ever owned," clearly grasped the importance of owning a property such as Alaska that significantly increased the size, influence and power of the United States.

Memory 3: "The Runaway"

A widow who lived on the edge of town had two "right smart" daughters, and one night Andy and another apprentice chunked (threw stones at) the girls' window. The indignant mother found out who the culprits were and threatened to "persecute." This was a serious threat, for erring apprentices could be handled sharply by the law. Rather then run the risk, Andy and brother Bill decamped, taking two other discontented apprentices with them. Heading south, they did not stop until they came to Carthage, a town fifty miles southwest of Raleigh. There they succeeded in obtaining the use of a shack and opened a tailoring business of their own. Selby promptly inserted an advertisement in the Raleigh Star, posting a reward for the recovery of the runaways, but perhaps by the typesetter's error the brothers' description was reversed:

Ten Dollar Reward

Ran away from the subscriber, two apprentice boys, legally bound, named William and Andrew Johnson. The former is of dark complexion, black hair, eyes, and habits. They are much of a height, about five feet four or five inches. The latter is very flashy, freckled face, light hair, and fair complexion. They went off with two other apprentices. When they went away they wore well-clad blue cloth coats, light homespun coats, and new hats. I will pay the above reward to any person who will deliver said apprentices to me in Raleigh, or I will give the above Reward for Andrew Johnson alone.

Evidently Selby thought that in losing the services of Bill he was not losing much; but Andrew, despite his alleged "black habits" was another matter. It is possible that Selby bore Andrew a grudge because of the lad's refusal to kowtow; the forms of servility he simply would not observe.
　　　　—*The First President Johnson*, by Lately Thomas, page 14.

In the memory, Johnson was on a hero's journey from the moment he first threw stones at the girls' window to the endless challenges and successes along the way. The rebellious fifteen-year-old runaway believed he could find his way through only by fighting back and making sure that he was beholden to no one. Remembering himself throwing stones was evidence of his hostility and how incensed he could become when he felt trapped or powerless. In ways that mattered emotionally, he continued to pursue power and revenge for the remainder of his life.

The memory encapsulated how Johnson responded to pressures and demands in an aggressive manner, regardless of the consequences. In part, this aggressiveness may have been the "black habits" to which Mr. Selby referred in his "wanted poster." Johnson reacted to the sting of each stone or injustice thrown at him by lashing out at others; he did this both to assert his dominance and to make sure that his rivals felt the sting of his own hostility. In a letter he wrote to a friend in 1845 he commented:

> *When I sum up the many taunts, the jeers, the gotten-up and intended slights to me and mine, all without cause so far as known, I wish from the bottom of my heart that we were all blotted out of existence, and even the remembrance of things that were.*

The angry fifteen-year-old in the memory carried his resentments throughout his life. Each real or perceived slight provoked him to do and say whatever was necessary to prevail. For instance, in running for reelection as Governor of Tennessee, Johnson remarked of his opponent, a member of the Know-Nothing Party, "Show me a Know-Nothing, and I will show you a loathsome reptile, on whose neck every honest man should set his feet." When members of his own Democratic Party asked him to moderate his vindictiveness, Johnson refused to back down, commenting, "Gentlemen, I will make that same speech tomorrow if it blows the Democratic Party to hell."

In 1862, President Lincoln appointed Johnson as the *military* Governor of Tennessee with the rank of Brigadier General. Johnson seized control of the Bank of Tennessee, shut down newspapers that opposed the Union and arrested citizens who refused to take a loyalty oath. His actions provoked the Mayor of Nashville to characterize his military command as "a reign of terror." As President, Johnson's bodyguard remembered him as "the best hater I ever knew." Moreover, according to biographer David O. Stewart, during the White House years, when an illness kept his wife Eliza in bed:

> *The president worked across the hall from her sick room, looking in on her during the day. She, in turn, tried to moderate his searing temper. A White House worker remembered her staving off eruptions by gently touching the President's arm and saying, "Now, Andrew."*

Johnson's political agenda was driven by the sense of outrage that was implied in the memory rather than sophisticated thinking. First, he began with the premise that the wealthy elite (such as Mr. Selby) were responsible for everything bad that happened to him. He proceeded to look for evidence that justified both his initial premise and his outrage at the privileged class. Johnson was more concerned with settling a score than he was in compromising. He once said, "Compromise! Let us have no more compromise! We have compromised and conservatized until there is hardly any Constitution left."

In his rush to vent his anger and demonize his opponents, he overlooked complexity and subtlety. His uncompromising manner worked reasonably well when he served at the state and federal level as a legislator, and as Governor of Tennessee. However, during his Presidency, Johnson's "us-versus-them" mentality threatened to tear the divided nation further apart.

Shortly after Lincoln's assassination, the Republicans were hopeful that a southern Democrat such as Johnson could unite North and South and lead the country from war to peace. Senator Benjamin Franklin Wade, a radical Republican who supported equal rights for African-Americans said, "Johnson we have faith in you—By the Gods, there will be no trouble in running the government." Nevertheless, it was only a matter of time before Johnson's inflexibility on issues such as the Black Codes and the Thirteenth Amendment alienated both moderate and radical Republicans. The same rebelliousness and hostility that defined his personality in the memory now characterized his relationships with Congress. For example:

- He used Executive Orders to push through his preferred causes rather than working with Congress. In bypassing Congress, he created a counter-reaction that ultimately led to his impeachment.

- He vetoed the Freedmen's Bureau and claimed that Republicans were "laboring to destroy the fundamental principles of government."

- He vetoed the Civil Rights Act, and when his veto was overturned he told his private secretary, "Sir, I am right. I know I am right and I am damned if I do not adhere to it." Historian David O. Stewart remarked, "The veto was for many his defining blunder, setting a tone of perpetual confrontation with Congress that prevailed for the rest of his presidency."

- He met with Senator Charles Sumner who tried to persuade Johnson to reconsider his views on Reconstruction. At the end of the meeting, Sumner reached for his hat to leave and realized that Johnson had used it as a spittoon for his tobacco juice.

- He toured the East and Midwest to generate support for his views on Reconstruction. The tour, or "swing around the circle" as it was called, engendered rancorous verbal battles in which Johnson shouted at the people in the audience. As historian William Seale remarked, "The president presented himself less as the friend of the people than as an angry man controlled by his own rages." During the tour, his impassioned but intemperate behavior resulted in the opposition winning an overwhelming victory in the congressional elections of 1866.

From Johnson's point of view, he was doing the humane and right thing regarding Reconstruction. In 1864, before Lincoln was re-elected, vice-presidential candidate Johnson told a crowd of former slaves: "I will indeed be your Moses and lead you through the Red Sea of war and bondage to a fairer future of liberty and peace." Perhaps Johnson could not follow through with this intention because he was still a slave to a memory in which whatever self-worth he had was due to the feeling that, at least, he was superior to the blacks. Johnson referred to Mr. Selby as "a harsh and cruel master." His ever-present reserve of malice for Selby—and the wealthy elite—poured forth freely in his actions and public statements. With the memory, Johnson was still grieving for himself and for the dignity he was denied as a child.

In this context, a passage in *Deuteronomy* has particular relevance: Moses addressed the next generation of Israelites that were about to enter the Promised Land: "Do not hate an Egyptian for you were a stranger in his land." In other words, if the Israelites had continued to hate their oppressors, Moses would have succeeded in leading them out of Egypt, but they would still have been slaves to their past memories of victimization. Likewise, although Johnson escaped his apprenticeship he never escaped his destructive anger and hostility. As a result, he was unable to empathize with the legitimate concerns of African-Americans, even though their histories were inextricably connected. A memory of unresolved grievances and victimization prevented Johnson from defending the victimized lest he be considered one of them.

Although Johnson did not commit a "high crime," his irascible personality and combativeness so alienated congress that they chose impeachment as a viable way to silence him. Johnson provided congress with the opportunity to impeach him for a misdemeanor when he violated the Tenure of Office Act by dismissing Secretary of War Edward M. Stanton from his cabinet without congressional approval. The House voted eleven Articles of Impeachment against him. In 1868, Johnson was tried by the Senate and was acquitted by a single vote. Historian John. W Burgess remarked:

> *He was utterly and entirely guiltless of the commission of any crime or misdemeanor. He was low-born and low-bred, violent in temper, obstinate, coarse, vindictive, and lacking in the sense of propriety, but he was not behind any of his accusers in patriotism and loyalty to the country, and in his willingness to sacrifice every personal advantage for the maintenance of the Union and the preservation of the Government.*

The above description of Johnson was very much in keeping with a memory in which he portrayed himself in opposition to the established order. He would not allow himself to be controlled in the memory and he would not allow Congress to control him as President. In the memory and as President, his motto seemed to be: "I would rather fight than give in!" The oppositional manner that the memory presaged contributed to Johnson's reputation as one of the unfortunate Presidents who was least able to forge a consensus with the Legislative branch.

The memory captured a fiery rage that Johnson could never extinguish. Moreover, the memory revealed his indomitable spirit—never to concede and to stand against injustice—whether as a teenager running away to avoid prosecution; as the only Southern congressman who was opposed to secession at the beginning of the Civil War; or as a devoted Unionist who faced violent mobs and death threats during the secession crisis as he traveled home to Tennessee to convince his fellow southerners to remain in the Union. A memory that portended trouble for anyone who dared to challenge him inspired the one-time tailor to try to mend the social and economic fabric of America by speaking truth to power.

Memory Four: "Touched by Love and Despair"

In Carthage, North Carolina, Andrew (age sixteen) found employment as a journeyman tailor. Carthage could not keep him for long, especially as he was always in danger of apprehension as long as he remained in North Carolina. So after a few months he walked on. This time he crossed the state line to settle in Laurens, South Carolina, where he found employment in a local tailor shop, and stayed for almost 2 years. But he soon had interests other than the mere drudgery of every day labor. He fell in love with a local girl named Mary Wood, whom he decided to woo. First he made a quilt for her; then he mustered enough courage to ask her for her hand. But he was turned down. Her mother could see no advantage in tying her daughter's fate to a penniless tailor. Deeply disappointed, Andrew left Laurens.

Anxious to clear his name, Johnson now returned to Raleigh. His old friend, Selby's former foreman, had opened a tailor shop of his own but could not employ his erstwhile companion because of Andrew's unfulfilled indenture. Selby was no longer in Raleigh; he had moved some twenty miles out into the country. Andrew paid a visit to his old master in the hope of coming to an agreement, but Selby was unreasonable. He would not allow his former apprentice to pay for his time without security, a sum of money Andrew could not obtain, and accordingly the dejected young man decided to leave North Carolina for good. As his friend Tom Lomsdon remembered it, he was wearing a little cap and carried a bundle of shirts and socks thrown over his shoulder. For about two miles Lomsdon walked out of town with him, Johnson talking all the time about the great things he was going to accomplish in the West. Then it was time to say goodbye. There were tears in his eyes, but he was determined to strike out on his own, across the mountains in Tennessee.

—Andrew Johnson; A Biography by Hans L Trefousse, pp. 23-24.

The memory encapsulated Johnson's despair. The two setbacks in the memory—being turned down by both the family of Mary Wood, regarding marriage, and Mr. Selby, regarding the dissolution the apprenticeship—served as reminders of what it felt like to be considered less worthy than others and to have both proposals rejected. He may have seemed like a low-life character to some, but this was a judgment Johnson also made of himself. Similarly, in *The Metamorphosis*, Franz Kafka described the story of Gregor Samsa, a hardworking salesman unappreciated by his employer, who awakens to find himself transformed into a bug. Like Gregor, Johnson's self-image was shaped by his consciousness of how others viewed him.

Burning with ambition but plagued by a lack of perceived control over his future, Johnson was a mix of brashness and insecurity. Insult to his pride was the fuel; anger was the fire. Conquering insecurity and controlling anger would be his greatest challenges—things he struggled with all his life. For example, as the military Governor of Tennessee with a rank of Brigadier General who subjugated his opposition, Johnson wrote a letter to his wife in 1862 in which he remarked, "I feel sometimes like giv[in]g up in dispare [despair]." In addition, a contemporary of Johnson described his life as an, "intense, unceasing, desperate upward struggle."

Determined to strike out on his own, Johnson left North Carolina and established a successful tailoring business in Greeneville, Tennessee. At the age of 18, he married 16-year-old Eliza McCardle, the daughter of a local shoemaker. They were married by Mordecai Lincoln, the first cousin of Thomas Lincoln, who was the father of Abraham Lincoln. Andrew and Eliza were married for nearly fifty years and had five children. Johnson's early personal and professional success was testament to his ability to work against the odds. In situations where he anticipated failure, the memory helped him to prepare for life's difficult and uncontrollable moments. Bouncing back from the setbacks he experienced helped him believe he could also bounce back in the future. In part, Johnson succeeded because he did not want to revisit the painful feelings of rejection that were described in the memory.

Johnson defended against his feelings of despair and victimization with an outward aggressiveness. He was filled with animosity toward the characters in the memory at whom he could not retaliate; so he retaliated against his political foes with all the passion of someone who wished to conceal his insecurity. Paradoxically, the dominating and fighting spirit that served him so well as a young adult only served to thwart him as President. Johnson's abrasive personality tended to undermine any possibility for compromise. This led historian James Ford Rhodes to comment, "No one else was so instrumental in defeating Johnson's own aims as was Johnson himself."

President Woodrow Wilson described Johnson's tendency to compete rather than cooperate as follows: "He was self willed, implacable, headstrong and tempestuous—he would yield nothing and alienate his very best friends by attacking Congress in public with gross insult and abuse, losing credit with everybody."

When Johnson felt vulnerable or threatened he could be triggered into acting like the very characters he despised in the memory. One possible reason Johnson and Mr. Selby did not reach an agreement to dissolve the apprenticeship was that they were too much alike. Selby was also a product of a place and time in which the deck was stacked against him. In order to survive in business, Mr. Selby had to be tough-minded and prudent about his "contractual rights." Johnson's own intractable manner was a reflection of how he perceived Mr. Selby as an uncompromising taskmaster. On one level, Mr. Selby was an adversary. On another level, he made Johnson feel better about himself as an aspiring tailor. In his rise from humble roots to the Presidency, Johnson embodied Mr. Selby's brashness, his willingness to fight for his rights and his conviction never to concede to the opposition. Both were self-made individuals, inflexible, merciless to those they opposed and a product of the times that made them. Mr. Selby was woven in the very fabric of Johnson's own mindset.

Summary

In George Orwell's essay "Revenge Is Sour" he observed, "Properly speaking, there is no such thing as revenge. Revenge is an act which you want to commit when you are powerless and because you are powerless; as soon as the sense of impotence is removed, the desire evaporates also." Throughout his life, Johnson was unable to escape his sense of powerlessness. From the time he was robbed of his self-esteem by Mr. Devereaux, Mr. Selby, and the family of Mary Wood, Johnson wanted to obtain enough power to crush others. He did this to compensate for his insufficiencies, disavow his feelings of powerlessness and retaliate for being looked down upon by his so-called betters. His overall insecurity showed itself in his intense hostility for the wealthy elite who, he imagined, were living what he had missed out on.

In the first memory, Johnson established a menacing mood that permeated his life like a discordant note. In the second memory, receiving the gift of *The American Speaker* provided Johnson with a lifelong love of learning and the will to pursue his improbable journey to the White House, even when he worried about appearing uneducated because he never went to school. The memory inspired Johnson to escape his lower-class standing, overcome the shame he felt at being considered poor and worthless, and distinguish himself from the other apprenticed boys with whom he labored twelve hours a day. The memory of receiving *The American Speaker* reinforced Johnson's belief that no dream was outside his reach if he believed in himself and his potential to succeed.

To survive the humiliation of his impoverished, indentured and unschooled childhood, Johnson called upon these memories to remind him never to forget his modest beginnings and early hardships. As a politician, Johnson championed the rights of working-class people; that the poor should not be used as pawns for the rich to achieve their ends. As he pointed out, "The people have never deserted me, and, God willing, I will never desert them." Fighting for the common man enabled him to work through his own childhood deprivations and move beyond them. Johnson was proud of his humble origins and the fighting spirit he demonstrated in overcoming obstacles. The memories were an affirmation that abject poverty and lack of education did not have to be an impediment to success, if one tried hard enough.

Mark Twain commented, "To arrive at a just estimate of a renowned man's character one must judge it by the standards of his time, not ours." Johnson's personal, social, and political standards were based on beliefs and attitudes embedded in the four memories. These beliefs and attitudes directed him to act in both a hostile and caring manner, but the hostile side too often predominated. As a result, according to historian David O. Stewart:

> *After the [Civil] war, at the most delicate moment in our history, when greatness of spirit was needed, the man from Tennessee could not be more than the forceful, intelligent, and intransigent politician he had always been. The times demanded more.*

Unfortunately, Johnson's memories demanded something different. He emerged from the tailor shop and rose to the White House, but he could not rise above some of the grievances, resentments and insecurities that were so powerfully symbolized in the memories. Whatever mistakes Johnson made during his Presidency, he truly believed that the United States needed to reform itself to better represent the interests of the working-class poor. In addition, he truly believed in the importance of demonstrating his contempt for all the traditional sources of power, from Mr. Selby to the Legislative branch that impeached him. These beliefs and attitudes were inspired by his memories.

As for why it is important to avoid the automatic conclusion that Johnson was a mean-spirited racist who presided over a disastrous presidency, an answer was suggested by Abraham Lincoln: In 1864, Lincoln remarked, "No man has a right to judge Andrew Johnson in any respect who has not suffered as much and done as much as he for the Nation's sake."

Bibliography

Burgess, John W. Reconstruction and the Constitution: 1866-1876, New York, Charles Scribner and Sons,1902.

Irelan, Robert, M.D. The Republic Or A history Of The United States Of America, Volume 18, Forgotten Books, 2012.

Means, Howard. The Avenger Takes His Place: Andrew Johnson and the 45 days that Changed the Nation. Harcourt, Inc. Orlando, 2006.
> *A thorough and provocative description of Johnson's character including a compelling history of his early life.*

Odegard, Dave. The Favorite Books of all 44 Presidents. https://www.buzzfeed.com/daveodegard/the-favorite-books-of-all-44-presidents-of-the-united-states?utm_term=.ttngBDlGl#.crrm2n1N1. Accessed Nov. 17, 2016.

Reed, Annette Gordon. Andrew Johnson. Times Books; Henry Holt and Company, N.Y., 2001.

Rhodes, James Ford. History of the United States, originally published by McMillan company, London, 1906. Antique Reprints, 2016.

Seale, William. The Presidents House. The White House Historical Association, 1986.

Stewart, David O. Impeached: The Trial of President Andrew Johnson and the Fight for Lincoln's Legacy. Simon and Schuster, New York, 2009.
> *A compelling and well researched account of Johnson's impeachment proceedings that provides a highly critical view of his presidential legacy.*

Thomas, Lately. The First President Johnson. William Morrow and Company, Inc., N.Y., 1968.

Trefousse, Hans L. Andrew Johnson: A Biography. W.W. Norton and Company, N.Y., 1989.

Rutherford B. Hayes

President of the United States
1877-1881

Memory One: "Family"

At the time of my first recollections, our family consisted of Mother, Fanny [Sister], Uncle Sardis [Birchard], Arcena Smith [Cousin], and myself. During these early years Uncle was regarded as the stay of the family and our protector and advisor in every trouble. He was appointed guardian of Fanny and myself, and during all our lives has been a father to us ... [Fanny] slept with Arcena and loved her dearly.
—Diary and Letters of Rutherford B. Hayes, Volume one, pp. 4-6.

The memory helped to shape Hayes' optimistic frame of mind and imbued him with a sincere commitment to family values. He viewed his family members as companions working together to support each other. His sister Fanny protected him as a feeble and sickly child and he protected her when she later became ill. Hayes' compassion and heartfelt satisfaction in helping Fanny presaged his give-and-take ethic as well as an overall concern for the welfare of others. The emphasis on family values in the memory sparked a lifelong interest in genealogy and prompted him years later to make several journeys to his first home in Ohio, along with a special interest in tracing his family tree. Biographer Harry Bernard remarked,

> *He knew that he was loved in his house, by his mother, by Fanny and by Arcena. They filled his world with affection. This love, above everything else, defined his later character. It was easy to see that, being the beneficiary of so much love in his family, he was able to have an attitude of goodwill toward almost everyone. He did not have to be miserly with love but could dispense it freely. Even then, as a child, he was grateful for it. "How I loved them" he explained as a grown-up.*

If Hayes' good will and interest in helping others began with his family, then as President, he and his wife Lucy would model family values. To this end, Rutherford and Lucy presented themselves as an ideal family by banishing alcohol from the White House. According to historian William Seale,

> *The Hayes cultivated their role as a model family. They visibly attended church as a family; dinners did not last much past ten; the familiar characteristics of the sporting life passed from the White House scene. In the wake of the glamorous Grants the Hayes' transformed customary procedures to make the White House conform to the new moral ideals of their time.*

Although Hayes was not personally opposed to drinking, liquor was prohibited to exemplify the importance of family values, as first expressed in the memory. After one official dinner, the Secretary of State quipped, "It was a brilliant affair; the water flowed like champagne!" The Hayes' emphasis on family values turned his wife into a celebrity. She was called "First Lady of the Land" as well as "Lemonade Lucy" and she became the first First Lady to graduate from college.

A memory in which Hayes celebrated family togetherness and support provided a prototype for how he would try to help the nation heal following the polarizing Presidential election of 1876, the one-hundredth anniversary of American independence. In the election, his opponent, Democrat Samuel J. Tilden, won the popular vote and was ahead in the Electoral College. Returns from three states—South Carolina, Louisiana and Florida, all controlled by Republicans—were in dispute. To resolve the issue, an electoral commission was established consisting of five senators, five representatives, and five Supreme Court justices. The commission voted 8-7 strictly along party lines to award all disputed states to Hayes.

Many Americans felt that the country had lost its way and some Democrats threatened open rebellion rather than accept the findings of the partisan commission. Hayes was called "The Fraudulent President" and "Ruther-fraud B. Hayes." Public disturbances were frequent, especially in Washington and there were threats of assassination. Under circumstances of widespread fear of violence,

President Grant insisted that Hayes take the oath of office in private at the White House. Instead of reducing the electorate to those who were for or against him, Hayes tried to treat the different factions as if they were one united family; replicating the familial generosity and kindness he recalled in the memory. It was Hayes' sensible, good-natured manner that balanced America's polarizing instincts during the turbulence of the post-election years. In an effort to heal a divided country, Hayes promised fairness and honesty even if it conflicted with the best interests of the Republican Party. In his inaugural address he remarked,

> *He serves his party best who serves his country best ... Let me assure my countrymen of the Southern States that it is my earnest desire to regard and promote their truest interest—the interests of the white and of the colored people both and equally—and to put forth my best efforts on behalf of a civil policy which will forever wipe out in our political affairs the color line and the distinction between North and South, to the end that we may have not merely a united North or a united South, but a united country.*

It was this magnanimous feeling and graciousness that typified Hayes' role as a politician and led to him being called, "Statesman of Reunion." As a politician Hayes respected the opposition and encouraged contrasting points of view. The memory prepared him to see the value of not only tolerating differences between a divided electorate but welcoming diversity as one of the great strengths of America. When all depended on National unity—sticking together and helping each other during a time of crisis—his inaugural comments provided an example of tolerance and represented someone who had confidence and faith in America's future—for Hayes this confidence was inspired by the message of cooperation in the memory.

Memory Two: "Mother"

We lived in a new two-story brick house. Our garden, grass plot, and barnyard occupied, I think, two village lots about twelve rods on

William Street by sixteen on Winter Street … We were well provided with all that was necessary for comfort and our red-brick house, built fronting on the street, was as grand as the houses of our neighbors Mother's income was derived from the rent of a good farm about ten miles north of town on the east side of the Whetstone. We received as rent one-third of the crops and half of the fruit, delivered at our barn and house in town. The great events of our childhood were connected with this farm. We visited it three or four times a year, each trip, occupying a whole day. Sugar-making, cider-making, cherry time, and gathering hickory nuts and walnuts were the occasions of these long looked for and delightful trips. Mother sometimes rode on horseback, carrying one and sometimes both of us on the horse behind her. Generally, however, we walked and crossed the river a short distance below the farm in a canoe. The tenants always were attentive to Fanny and myself. They gave us colored eggs filled with sugar at Easter, pet birds, squirrels, rabbits, quail's eggs, turtle's eggs, and other curious gifts easily found in the country at that time.
　　—*Diary and Letters of Rutherford B. Hayes*, Volume one, pp. 4-6.

The vivid details and images of Hayes' home landscape never left him. If an earliest memory is the first draft of self-identity, then remembering a pleasant landscape is the first and most lasting visual impression of this consciousness. Throughout his life Hayes strove to become a personable and approachable individual who mirrored the harmony and peacefulness of his home's exterior. The landscape provided an image of serenity through the lens of nature and left a permanent mark in Hayes' memory; such details may skate on the surface but the power they possess deserves closer examination.

Hayes used the ambience of the landscape as a counterpoint to his own impressions of life, others and himself. The memory was the beginning of his recognition of the influence that each family member had on him. One imagines young Hayes wandering through the garden or the farm asking himself questions such as: How did I become the person I am? How am I influenced by my family? How should I handle conflict within my family? What are my family values and how should I apply them outside my home? The challenge of the memory was to reconcile himself to his family—the people who mattered most in his life. When Hayes thought about his family, he experienced the sounds and smells of the garden, the touch of the flowers and the birds chirping all over again. As an adult with an excellent education, a stellar record in the military and an accomplished lawyer and politician, Hayes used the memory to compare himself now with who he was and where he came from many years earlier.

During his professional career, Hayes and his wife shared a great interest and affection for gardening. They cultivated the groves and flower gardens at their Ohio estate and they developed a gardening program after moving to the White House. In the memory, Hayes recalled delightful trips to his family farm in which he was given "colored eggs filled with sugar at Easter." This landscape detail takes on additional meaning in light of the fact that Hayes began the tradition of rolling Easter eggs on the White House lawn. Easter egg-rolling has been an annual event at the White House ever since. In a way, an image from the memory took on a life of its own in the White House—memories sometimes have a way of installing themselves into the present.

The beauty of Hayes' garden, grass plot and farm spoke to him through the mood it evoked and the positive associations it generated. It took painstaking effort, planning and hours of hard labor to cultivate a landscape whose component parts worked together to bring about a beautiful harmony. Similarly, as a lawyer, politician and general, Hayes was attentive to the task at hand. He dedicated himself to working with others in a cooperative manner to keep the flame of collegiality going. Landscape images from the memory provided Hayes with self-confidence and lifted his spirits as he prepared the necessary groundwork to face the world. Part of the implied message of the imagery was that he sprung from the soil, stayed true to his Ohio roots and grew into history.

Memory Three: "Fanny and Uncle Sardis"

My earliest recollection of Fanny is as my protector and nurse when I was a sickly, feeble boy, three or four years old. She would lead me carefully about the garden and barnyard and on short visits to the nearest neighbors. She was loving and kind to me and very generous...

With the grown persons in the family [Fanny] was at this time quick-tempered and obstinate. Uncle [Sardis], to tease her, would put her on the mantel-piece and tell her she must stay there until she asked him to take her down. This she would not do, but sitting perfectly upright to avoid falling, her face flushed with anger, she would bid him defiance, and rarely if ever give up.

The first important incident of her life, which I recollect, was a long and severe illness in the summer of 1827. At one time her life was despaired of, and for many weeks she was dangerously sick. After the disease (dysentery) left her, she was a long time regaining her strength. It was in the summer during the warmest weather. After she was able to sit up, I daily gave her little rides upon a small hand-sled which with great difficulty I hauled about the garden. We were both very happy. I can remember no happier days in childhood then these.
    —*Diary and Letters of Rutherford B. Hayes*, Volume one, pp. 4-6.

Hayes was born October 4,1822 in Delaware, Ohio, the youngest of four children, two of which died in childhood. His father operated a successful farm and whiskey distillery in Ohio but died ten weeks before Rutherford was born. Raised by his mother Sophia, "Rud" as he was called, struggled during infancy. His mother remarked, "For two years I had little hope of his life." When Hayes was three years old, his brother, Lorenzo drowned in a skating accident on a frozen pond. The death of his brother influenced his mother to be even more protective of her sickly youngest son. During his early years, Hayes was home-schooled and was not allowed to play outside. As a result, he developed an exceptionally close relationship to his sister, Fanny, who was two years older. Hayes was profoundly affected by their companionship, as noted in the memory, and later recalling:

Oh, her beautiful character, her winning ways—her sweet affections! She loved me as an only sister loves a brother whom she imagines almost perfect, and I loved her as an only brother loves his sister who is perfect.

During his childhood, the presence of his mother's brother, Uncle Sardis Birchard, provided Hayes with a father figure who throughout his life would help Hayes with his education, legal career and business ventures. Hayes completed his preparatory studies in 1838 and then attended Kenyon College in Gambier, Ohio, instead of Yale, which his uncle had urged him to attend. Perhaps in contesting his uncle he revealed the same maverick tendencies that Fanny demonstrated in the memory. Hayes was the Valedictorian at Kenyon and in the fall of 1843 he attended Harvard Law School. In 1852, while practicing law in Cincinnati, Ohio, he married Lucy Webb. His wife influenced him to attend religious services regularly with her—though he never joined a church—and to become an anti-slavery advocate and a teetotaler following their move to the White House.

Hayes compensated for having been a sickly and feeble child with the support, assistance and protection of his older sister. Subsequently in adulthood he obtained the support of friends and colleagues through his charm, independence and resourcefulness. Nevertheless, growing up in an over-protective home led to a state of anxiety which Hayes later described as "nervous to the verge of disaster—going to pieces on the slightest provocation." Neighbors during this period referred to him as "timid as a girl." His conflicted emotional state could be understood by the contrast between a happy, loving family and a fear that he would one day lose his mind, as there was a history of mental illness in his family. He revealed that his fear of mental instability came from knowing "a number of near relatives on both my mother's and father's side of the house having become insane."

Hayes' insecurities continued throughout his adolescence. At the age of nineteen he remarked,

> *I have always been ambitious dreaming of future glory, of performing some virtuous or patriotic action, but it has been all dreams, and no reality. From my earliest recollection, I have thought I had great power in me, yet at the same time I was fully satisfied of my present insignificance and mental*

> *weakness. I have imagined that at some future time I could do*
> *considerable, but the more I learn, the more I feel my littleness.*

After Hayes assumed the Presidency, following the bitterly disputed 1876 election, he remarked, "I shall show a grit that will astonish those who predict weakness." Showing "grit" was a continuation of an attitude that was first revealed in the memory, that is, demonstrating to his sister the same warmth, determination and protectiveness that she showed to him when he was in need. The message of being helped by Fanny reminded him of his vulnerable beginnings, while the message of helping Fanny reminded him of the power of grit and persistence in transforming himself from a position of infirmity to a position of protector.

In helping his sister, Hayes discovered an elevating and consoling truth: his sister made him feel compassionate; and as a Harvard educated lawyer practicing in Cincinnati, Ohio, from 1858 to 1861, he extended this compassion to the people of Cincinnati as well as his clients. For example, the giving and compassionate spirit revealed in the memory paved the way for Hayes to provide legal aid when the Underground Railroad called upon his services. He later recalled, "there was a period when I never went to bed without expecting to be called out."

In addition, his actions as a defense lawyer in three murder trials marked him as a person of compassion who tried to find something positive or redeeming in his clients to support their defense. One case involved a woman who had poisoned a number of her employers. Hayes emphasized the defendant's mental state and extenuating circumstances: her mother believed herself to be the bride of Jesus Christ as well as a Mormon prophetess; and her father had been a drunkard who committed suicide. Hayes argued for an insanity defense, commenting:

> *The calamity of insanity is one which may touch very nearly*
> *the happiness of the best of our citizens. We all know that in*
> *one of its thousand forms it has carried grief and agony*
> *unspeakable into many a happy home, and we must all wish to*
> *see such rules in regard to it established as would satisfy an*

intelligent man if, instead of this friendless girl, his own sister or daughter were on trial. And surely to establish such rules will be a most notable achievement of that intelligence and reason which God has given to you, but he has denied to her whose fate is in your hands.

Hayes saved the woman from the gallows, instead being committed to a mental institution.

In part, Hayes dealt with his insecurities and fears by stepping back and becoming an observer of human nature—demonstrating a concern and empathy for the thoughts, feelings and problems of others. To this end, Hayes inserted himself in the memory as an observer in what appeared to be a minor if not amusing interaction between Fanny and Uncle Sardis. Two people, both believing they were right, kept talking past each other. Hayes's critical detachment elicited a sense of calm, allowing him to avoid alarm or panic during stressful situations. Being a neutral third-party enabled him to identify with each opposing viewpoint; to harmonize the different accounts with one another; and to maintain a sense of loyalty and love for both his sister and uncle without taking sides. Hayes wanted to see himself in an elevated manner; he wanted to be as objective, compassionate and understanding as he imagined each family member would be to him under similar circumstances. In short, Hayes learned from the memory a logical first step for getting along in any situation—if you do not know what to say or do, step back, observe and keep your thoughts to yourself.

Hayes' own identity emerged in contrast to how he perceived Fanny and Uncle Sardis. Both represented two different ways of interacting and provided a mirror into competing aspects within Hayes's own personality. Fanny responded in the moment; she was straightforward, spontaneous and defiant. Moreover, she stood in contrast to Hayes' more conforming, reserved and restrained approach to life. Uncle Sardis represented the settled world of conventions; whereas Fanny represented the unsettled world of self-assertion and boldness. Fanny was prepared to fight and Uncle Sardis was prepared to adapt.

If a supportive father figure with whom Hayes identified could provoke his beloved sister, then perhaps the uncle's actions reminded him of his own provocative tendencies—tendencies that he first manifested during his childhood:

> *When I was from nine to twelve years old we had many little quarrels, she always having the better with her tongue and I with my fists. This was a singular fact in our lives. I remember how I feared her ridicule. We loved each other dearly and yet behaved as if we were hateful enough.*

The opposing tendencies in Fanny and Uncle Sardis reflected a divide within Hayes. A divide between traditional ways such as following the rules and living within the safety and security found in a loving home; and nontraditional ways such as challenging established authority and expressing strong emotions. When sixteen-year-old Hayes was enrolled at Kenyon College these opposing tendencies collided. Although he finished first in his class and was praised by the College, "For strength of mind, clearness of perception and soundness of judgment," he often defied school regulations. Hayes recalled:

> *We were forbidden to have any guns but I always had two. There were also strict rules against cooking in the rooms, but we cooked and I had considerable of a reputation as a cook.*

Ultimately, these competing tendencies were not mutually exclusive but rather co-equal wellsprings of inspiration. In Fanny, he became a bold advocate for progressive ideals such as equal treatment without regard to race; improvement through education and civil service reform; and in Uncle Sardis he became a compassionate conservative who expected compliance with established authority. For instance, during his Presidency, to root out corruption and promote civil service reform, Hayes sought to make appointments based on merit instead of political connections. The spoils system, he remarked "Ought to be abolished—let appointments and removals be made on business principles and fixed rules."

When members of Hayes' own Republican Party resisted his non-partisan efforts to reform the federal bureaucracy, Hayes defiantly issued an executive order that prevented federal workers from holding posts in political organizations at the same time. When New York City Customs Collector and future President Chester A. Arthur openly refused to comply with the executive order to quit his partisan political activities, Hayes removed this fellow Republican from his position. In this example, Hayes integrated his conventional and progressive tendencies in an effort to initiate civil service reform.

Hayes himself recognized the conflicting aspects within his own personality, remarking, "I am a radical in thought and a conservative in method." The ongoing conflict was that he so thoroughly identified with both Fanny and Uncle Sardis that he could never comfortably belong in either camp. Hayes knew intuitively that the roles of his sister and uncle were intertwined in a kind of mutual wholeness. From that he blended aspects of spontaneity and restraint to form a synthesis that marked him as a compromising and moderate person.

General Hayes of the Twenty-Third Ohio Regiment

Hayes was elected solicitor of Cincinnati in 1858, and in 1860 he served as vice-chairman of the Republican Executive Committee of Hamilton County. He was thirty-eight and without any military experience when the Civil War started in 1861. He joined a unit of Ohio volunteers called the Burnett Rifles who made him their captain. According to biographer Ari Hoogenboom, Hayes emerged as an "honest, humane, confident, resourceful, brave and determined officer." He was by his own modest description, "One of the good colonels in the great army."

His adolescent dream "of future glory, of performing some virtuous or patriotic action" came to fruition during the Civil War. Serving in the army became an extension of this dream as well as an extension of the positive relationship that he shared with his family. "How I love the Twenty-third" Hayes remarked, reflecting the spirit of family, devotion and comradeship that was implied in the memory. The depth of his familial association with the Twenty-Third is revealed in his diary entry after returning from leave with his family. Getting back to his unit "Felt like getting home." Future President William McKinley—who served with Hayes in the Twenty-third— captured this sense of family identification when he remarked about Hayes:

> *And he was always with you. He kept near to you in peace as he was close to you in war. He was never above his comrades. I heard him once say that the Grand Army button he wore on his coat was the grandest decoration he had ever had.*

Hayes provided the kind of fatherly treatment that inspired devotion and loyalty in his soldiers. According to biographer T. Harry Williams,

> *Hayes openly told his men he regarded them as children, his children, and they liked the idea of this relationship because they liked him. A Jewish soldier once came to Hayes to ask to transfer to another company. The men in his unit were ridiculing his religion, and he wanted to be in a certain company that contained a number of Jews. Hayes accomplished the change, and this man never forgot it. Even after suffering eight bullets through his body, he insisted on coming back to serve under the colonel.*

The need to acknowledge and deal with opposing aspects within himself may have predisposed Hayes toward acknowledging and dealing with entrenched barriers between military members and volunteers. Striving to be a substitute father figure—as Uncle Sardis was to him—required character traits such as empathy and a leadership style that emphasized "Leading from the Heart." Breaking down the military-versus-volunteer mentality came naturally to someone whose memory of helping and being helped by Fanny highlighted that "one serves one's self best by serving others first."

Hayes earned the admiration of his soldiers, not just by treating them as if they were extended family but also because they respected his courageousness and resolute manner in battle. One of his officers wrote:

This implicit trust in the man extended down through the brigade, the different regiments constituting it, and thence on down to the shortest man in the rear rank. We all knew no foolish movement would be ordered but wherever we were our leader was a leader in the full acceptance of the term, and we always found him well to the front, with the orders, "Come on boys," not "Go on boys."

Future President William McKinley—who served with Hayes in the Twenty-Third Regiment remarked: "His whole nature seemed to change when in battle. From the sunny, agreeable, the kind, the generous, the gentle gentleman he was, when the battle was once on, he was intense and ferocious." General Ulysses S. Grant praised Hayes for "conspicuous gallantry" and General John C. Fremont commented, "He is a hero. All his words and actions inspire enthusiasm and confidence." Hayes was wounded five times and had four horses shot out from under him. He was given the Brevet Medal as Major General of volunteers in 1865 "For gallant and meritorious services in the battles of Opequon, Fisher's Hill, and Cedar Creek."

After the War, Hayes served in the U.S. Congress from 1865 to 1867 as a Republican. Hayes left Congress to run for Governor of Ohio and was elected to two consecutive terms from 1868 to 1872, and then to a third term, from 1876 to 1877. In between 1872 and 1876, Hayes had planned to retire and spend more time with his family, having had two children born in the previous five years. But he was recruited to run for his old House seat in 1872; he agreed, but lost that election. He was reelected for a third term as Governor of Ohio in 1876. As Governor, his most important accomplishments included ratifying the 15th Amendment—which eliminated race as a qualification for voting—the establishment of Ohio State University, appointing nonpartisan boards to oversee state institutions and promoting education, prison and mental health reform.

Lucy Webb Hayes

In part, our memories direct our intentions. In Hayes' memory, he is telling himself that there is nothing more satisfying than helping someone who has the key to your heart. His loving relationship with his sister influenced his perspective and response to his subsequent relationship with his wife, Lucy Webb Hayes. In the end, the memory was a love story to his family that foreshadowed his loving and successful thirty-seven-year marriage. Rutherford and Lucy had eight children, three of whom would die in childhood.

Together Rutherford and Lucy compensated for each other's weaknesses and borrowed from each other's strengths. The memory transmitted intense emotions and revealed how Hayes was transformed from someone who found certainty in his status as a weak and feeble child, to someone who found certainty in a helping, caring and loving relationship. In the memory, Hayes saw himself in the most dramatic visible stage of his personal transformation.

As an adult, the memory served as a model for Hayes to help and love his wife in the same way he helped and loved his sister so many years earlier. In Lucy, he found someone who shared the spirit of cooperation and goodwill that typified his sister. For instance, even during their engagement, Lucy helped impoverished families, a passion that would come to define her life when she married Rutherford in 1852. During the Civil War, Lucy ministered to the needs of the sick and wounded during many camp visits, winning the admiration of the troops. Until her death in 1889, she was an advocate for welfare causes, promoted the value of education for both sexes and was a proponent of family values such as temperance. The portrait of her that hangs in the White House was commissioned by the Women's Christian Temperance Union.

Both Rutherford and Lucy shared the belief that good deeds represented more than an obligation or a sacrifice—they were a calling. Together they focused on good citizenship, national unity and balancing good deeds and family values with their politically progressive tendencies. After her death, Hayes wrote:

> *Few men in this most important relation of life have been as blessed as I have been. From early mature manhood to the threshold of old-age I have enjoyed her society in the most intimate of all relations. A better wife I never hope to have.*

On the Ledge of the Mantlepiece

In Memory Three, Hayes used the presence of Fanny as a symbol of bold and contentious behavior, in order to activate his own aggressive and daring side. He needed someone like Fanny to create the conditions under which he would let his own "lightning out of the bottle," such as asserting his independence from his overprotective mother. Conversely, he used the presence of Uncle Sardis as a symbol of traditional norms or conventional wisdom, in order to activate his own wish to subdue individuals who violated or pushed the limits. The memory was a wake-up call—that you cannot have it both ways. It was his responsibility to recognize and integrate discordant parts of his personality, lest he end up living "on the edge" (or on the ledge of the mantlepiece, as the case may be) in a dangerous situation.

One constant with memories is that there is often tension between what a person wants to remember (the parts that enhance self-image, such as helping Fanny) and what they should remember (valuable advice from the unconscious about errors in judgment such as being quick-tempered and obstinate). As an adult, by clever omissions and changes of emphasis Hayes could adjust the details so as to produce a memory that gives the impression of him being helpful and optimistic, or one that gives the impression of him being vulnerable to quick- tempered and obstinate behavior. This memory illustrates that point.

Hayes took pride in the fact that he was able to transform himself from a person who needed help to a person who provided it. His success came as a result of his willingness not to be bound by others' perceptions or expectations of him—such as his mother's over-protectiveness due to her fears regarding his frailty and safety. In part, the memory cultivated an optimistic frame of reference to motivate him to offset any negativity that he or others had about his status as a sickly, feeble child.

It was this same optimistic frame of reference that Hayes used as a colonel to motivate his officers. For instance, in 1862 Hayes was involved in a battle at Pack's Ferry. According to biographer T. Harry

Williams, there were "Conflicting reports that stated that the enemy was attacking in force and that the enemy was not attacking in force." Essentially, Hayes decided to hope for the best and prepare for the worst. He dispatched his soldiers for battle, placed the band in front of them, and told his men:

> *Fighting battles is like courting the girls: those who make most pretension and are boldest usually win. So, go ahead, give good hearty yells as you approach the ferry, let the band play. But don't expose yourselves, keep together and keep under cover.*

The history of warfare, of course, contains countless examples of officers who were required to play defense as well as offense. In this case, Hayes was inspired by a memory in which he triumphed against the odds by convincing himself that he could mobilize all the positives in his life and, through sheer determination, convert his weaknesses into strengths. He carried forward this optimistic spirit to motivate his soldiers and send the message that they were in control of their own fate. You feel empowered, so you act powerful. The strategy worked and the opposing forces retreated as Hayes' regiment approached. In the memory and in battle, Hayes generated optimism to allay initial doubt and heighten confidence.

Reconstruction and Indian Affairs

Perhaps there were times when Hayes was too invested in an optimistic frame of reference. In the memory, his determination and resolve allowed him to beat the odds; but eventually—in the case of Reconstruction—it prevented him from adapting to changing conditions and complex realities. Hoping for resolution, Hayes agreed to bring Reconstruction to an end. In 1877, he directed the Secretary of War "to see that the proper orders are issued for the removal of said troops from the State House." Subsequently, when the last soldiers were removed from the final State House, Reconstruction came to an end.

President Hayes remarked, "My policy is trust, peace, and to put aside the bayonet." Although he was optimistic and hoped for national unity, Southern white Democrats took control of their state governments with pernicious consequences for Southern blacks. Through nearly the next century, African-Americans were subjected to Jim Crow laws that afforded them the status of second-class citizens. In part, Hayes' misguided perception of the southern power structure was shaped by his desire and expectation that all sides would eventually come together in the spirit of national unity. Moreover, Hayes did not deal aggressively with Southern white Democrats, because doing so would have disrupted the fragile political alliance that had secured his presidency.

His detached objectivity and hope for the best approach—characteristics manifested in the memory—made it difficult for his own Republican Party to secure major concessions from Democrats on obtaining and safeguarding civil rights for African-Americans. In short, he was unable to convince the South to embrace racial equality or to appropriate funds to enforce the civil rights laws.

One could question whether Hayes contributed to a century of civil rights inequality by assuming positions of benign neglect and hoping that others would "do the right thing." Did Hayes assume these positions because he was influenced by the memory? Did Hayes' actions reflect his opposing tendencies—a progressive thinker who possessed the conservative instinct to suppress his more "radical" beliefs? Or was Hayes shaped by political and social circumstances beyond his control? It is likely that parts of all of these factors were contributory.

In the area of Indian affairs, the clarity of Hayes' self-observation, "I am a radical in thought and a conservative in method" was evident. While he articulated support for Native American citizenship rights, the United States military continued its advances into Indian territory. On the one hand, he advocated for peace and assumed the same kind of fatherly role he played as a Colonel during the War, such as preventing the removal of Native Americans to the Indian Territory; encouraging assimilation into white culture through education; and dividing Indian land into individual allotments. Overall, Native Americans received more humane treatment then ever before on their reservations. On the other hand, the Crow,

Blackfoot and Ute tribes were removed from their reservations and the Nez Perce were invaded after gold was discovered on their land.

Accomplishments

Though Hayes did not complete all he wanted to in office, given the challenges he faced with the economy, social and political divisions between North and South, and entrenched special interests, his overall record was solid. He vetoed the Bland-Allison Act in favor of preserving the gold standard; used federal money for infrastructure improvements to rebuild the south; implemented civil service reform emphasizing competence over loyalty; ordered federal troops to stop the Great Railroad Strike of 1877; initiated a trade agreement with China regulating immigration to the United States; strengthened border security with Mexico; proposed an amendment prohibiting re-elections of Presidents and extending their term to six years: and initiated an Indian policy that divided their land into individual allotments and promoted education.

These accomplishments were a result of his progressive tendencies and his willingness to compromise and negotiate with his opponents. It also helped that Hayes was a likable person, generous of spirit, inclusive and optimistic. According to biographer Harry Barnard, Hayes was "A perfect model of the conservative gentleman in politics—never doctrinaire, never extreme right or left."

During his post-presidential years, Hayes became one of the most active ex-Presidents in the country's history. Still influenced by the memory, he followed his own advice: a former president should "Like every good American citizen, be willing and prompt to bear his part in every useful work that will promote the welfare and happiness of his family, his town, and his country."

Additional accomplishments included that Hayes served as a Trustee of the Peabody Fund for the Education of Colored Children—as well as for Ohio State University and other Ohio colleges—and advocated for educational charities for all children. He supported civil and human rights that set a model for the thirty-ninth president, Jimmy Carter, during his post-presidential years.

Hayes' obituary in the *New York Times* in 1893 read:

> *The purity of his private and personal life was never questioned, and during his term of office at Washington there was a distinct elevating of the tone and standard of official life. There is no doubt that his Administration served a very useful purpose in the transition from sectional antagonism to national harmony, and from the old methods of dealing with the public service as party spoils to the new method of placing ascertained merit and demonstrated fitness above party service or requirements.*

Summary

A zest for life showed through in the memory. Hayes looked for the positive, celebrated life and came across as a mellow, centered and happy child. By outlining a generally optimistic outlook in the memory, he offered a preview of how he would later generate an attitude of goodwill and cooperation as a student, lawyer, general, congressman, governor and president. Hayes was a model of dignified and exemplary service for the public good. A contemporary who served with him in Congress commented, "He was one of the most patient, courteous and considerate public officials with whom I ever came in contact." His moderation and lack of pretense helped him to maintain positive relationships across the political spectrum.

If life and others are viewed in a positive manner and with a hopeful spirit, it is more likely to create the conditions in which one's expectations are realized. Hayes never forgot the place and home in which he was born and raised—the crux of his identity—even vivid details of the landscape stayed with him. Each family member influenced him in a positive direction and set the pattern for how he would subsequently interact with others outside of his family. The extent to which Hayes came across as centered—given the frailty he faced as a child—was a tribute to the transformational power of the memory—a memory in which he first recognized the value of kindness, support and loyalty that continued to influence him throughout his life.

Hayes's attempt to reconcile influences from Fannie and Uncle Sardis—fusing conservative thoughts with progressive elements—produced a well-rounded leader in whom a divided electorate could find a source of pride and security. Influenced by his memory of Fanny, perhaps Hayes overreached in the area of civil service reform and exposed himself to backlash for being too progressive. On the other hand, influenced by his memory of Uncle Sardis, he under-reached in the area of Reconstruction, exposing himself to backlash as an enabler for Southern white Democrats unwilling to provide equal rights for African-Americans. In part, whichever of the two visions prevailed at any one time determined his course of action.

Once, after reading Aristotle, Hayes remarked, "Virtue is defined to be mediocrity, of which either extreme is vice." At the end of his life, he questioned his middle-ground approach, commenting, "In avoiding the appearance of evil I am not sure but I have sometimes unnecessarily deprived myself and others of innocent enjoyments." Thus, it is much later in life that he recognized the need to measure himself against his own unique characteristics and then synthesize accordingly.

Hayes may not have been considered a great President but he was an exemplar of one with a loving heart, a devoted wife and family, a stellar military and political career, and emotional stability. Perhaps these accomplishments—inspired by the three memories—constitute his greatest triumph. Advocating for the insanity defense as a lawyer, fighting battles as a colonel, promoting equality as a politician, Hayes left an indelible impression upon America. Similarly, the memory left an indelible impression upon him by summoning his humane values, fending off his fears and demonstrating that the way forward lay in the simple act of helping and giving to others.

Hayes was deeply saddened by the death of his wife, Lucy, in 1889. He died from complications of a heart attack in 1893. His last words were, "I know I am going where Lucy is."

Bibliography

Barnard, Harry Rutherford B. Hayes and his America. Bobbs-Merrill Company, Inc, New York 1954.

Hoogenboom, Ari   The Presidency of Rutherford B Hayes. University Press of Kansas, 1988.

Hoogenboom, Ari   Rutherford B Hayes "One of the Good Colonels." McWhiney Press, 1999.

Seale, William   The President's House Volume 5. White House historical Association, 1986.

Trefousse, Hans L. Rutherford B. Hayes. Times Books, Henry Holt and Company, New York, 2002.

Williams, Charles Richard (editor) 5 volumes. Diary and Letters of Rutherford B. Hayes, 19th President of the United States. Columbus: Ohio State Archaeological and Historical Society, 1914.
> *These volumes bring together the entire spectrum of his concerns from childhood to the Presidency. A revealing exploration of his thoughts and feelings.*

Williams T. Harry   Hayes of the Twenty-Third: The Civil War Volunteer Officer. New York: Alfred A. Knopf, 1965.
> *The author brings to life the details of Hayes's career as an officer and explores their meaning as it relates to his military acumen, leadership and personality.*

Wise, John S. Recollections of Thirteen Presidents. Freeport, New York: Books for Libraries Press,1968.

James A. Garfield

President of the United States
March - September 1881

Memory One: *"Sea Struck."*

In 1848 Garfield left his rural home in Ohio against his mother's wishes to start a new life as a sailor on the open seas. He set out for Cleveland "with the firm intention of beginning at the bottom of the business of sailing and carefully mastering it." Upon arriving, none of the sailing vessels were at the docks except one owned by a drunken captain, who promptly cursed and belittled Garfield for being a sea-struck sixteen-year-old:

"Such swearing and cursing as he indulged in had never been my lot to hear before. He did not deign to answer my question. At the close of a time which must have been very short, but which seemed to me very long, I turned upon my heel and left the vessel amid the loud jeers and laughter of the men."
> —Life and Letters of Garfield, Volume One page 21.

The memory revealed Garfield's fragile self-confidence—powerfully symbolized in the image of "turning upon my heel and leaving the vessel" —and foreshadowed how it would ultimately shape his future actions and beliefs. For instance, Historian William A. Degregorio remarked:

> *As a young adult he experienced a prolonged period of mental depression, a period he later referred to as his "years of darkness." Similarly after his election as president, but before the inauguration, he was overcome with a sense of foreboding. He complained of severe headaches. He began having nightmares of being naked and lost.*

Perhaps the humiliation that was at the heart of the memory was also at the heart of his "years of darkness." The shame of being called out and ridiculed by the drunken captain may have led to a self-deprecating manner and a need to protect his fragile self-identity. Everything he accomplished afterwards was tainted by self-doubt and the need for approval from others. Driven by a wounded ego, no amount of success could compensate for his sense of insecurity. Garfield himself commented, "I so much despise a man who blows his own horn that I go to the extreme of not demanding what is justly my do." In addition, he developed an aversion to self-promotion or what he called "place-seeking" which became, he said, "the law of my life." In one case, Garfield regretfully told a friend, "I don't suppose I shall ever get the credit I deserve for my intellectual work."

Disturbing feelings from the memory may have reminded him of other humiliating childhood events that he did not wish to disclose or document. Accordingly, prior to the age of seventeen, documentation concerning his childhood comes mostly from his mother in letters she wrote to him and from direct interviews with her. However, as an adult, Garfield wrote several letters describing his "very bad" childhood which indicated that even before the memory took place, he felt negativistic, insecure and cheated by life. For instance, in a letter he wrote to his mother in 1854, he stated, "Cold hearted men frowned upon me and I was made the ridicule and sport of boys that had fathers, and enjoyed the luxuries of life."

In another letter he wrote to J. H. Rhodes in November, 1862, he stated:

> *To some men the fact that they come up from poverty and single-handedness is a matter of pride—I lament sorely that I was born to poverty—and in this chaos of childhood seventeen years passed before I caught up any inspiration which was worthy of my manhood—precious seventeen years in which a boy with a father and some wealth might have become fixed in manly ways—let no man praise me because I was poor and without a helper. It was very bad for my life.*

The letters bristle with regret and a deeply-held sense of being victimized. They are a stinging criticism of life, others and himself all in one—and his self-worth was a reflection of how he had been treated. Perhaps the memory—in which he boldly asserted himself by running away from home to seek adventure—helped him to look back at the other "undocumented" humiliating events of his childhood from a position of detached strength rather than weakness. Although Garfield did not disclose specific instances of his "very bad" childhood his subsequent beliefs and attitudes were shaped by their demoralizing legacy.

James Abram Garfield was born in a log cabin in Orange, Cuyahoga County, Ohio, November 19, 1831, the youngest of three living children. His father, Abram Garfield moved the family to Ohio in 1830 and settled in what was then known as "The Wilderness." Abram Garfield was a frontier farmer and a canal construction worker who died when James was an infant. A fire had broken out near the Garfield cabin; and after spending the entire day trying to save his property the elder Garfield returned exhausted to his cabin and soon died from pneumonia.

After her husband's death, Eliza Garfield raised her young family alone with help from her husband's half-brother. In 1842, when James was eleven years old, his mother remarried but left her new husband after living with him for a year. He later divorced her for desertion. According to biographer Alan Peskin:

> *Many years later, even after he had been elected President, and could be expected to view his childhood humiliations with detachment, Garfield received the news of his step-father's death with cold satisfaction—noting in his diary: "After this long, long silence ended in death it is hard for me to think of the man without indignation."*

The question implied in the memory was whether he would harness his resentments and use them as positive motivation—or whether he would succumb to his "darker" instincts. The drunken captain represented the darker side from which Garfield acted out his repressed anger. The sea-struck, ambitious adolescent represented his struggle to find a sense of purpose and meaning in an unfair and cruel world. In later years, Garfield referred to his "chaos of childhood." Given this perspective, the memory may have helped him to better examine his own internal contradictions.

In the end, Garfield's resentments both motivated and defeated him. On one hand, he sublimated his grievances by connecting his self-worth to the goal of serving others. His compassionate and humanistic side was revealed in the following remark he made as an adult: "I never meet a ragged boy in the street without feeling that I may owe him a salute, for I know not what possibilities may be buttoned up under his coat."

Perhaps Garfield thought that all that separated him from other impoverished youth was "fate" or the "Grace of God." His wounded heart tugged at him as he thought about the lives of others and their futures. In the belief that the highest good was to serve others and replace insult with forgiveness, he once remarked,

> *We should do nothing for revenge, but everything for security: nothing for the past; everything for the present and the future.*

On the other hand, he occasionally acted in a manner that was inconsistent with his altruistic goals. During his childhood, his mother described him as a "stubborn, willful boy," and it was reported by others that he could act in an aggressive and belligerent manner. During his college days, he agonized over behaving in an errant manner and straying outside a proper religious path. He wrote in his journal,

> *I am not enough devoted to the cause of Jesus of Nazareth. May the Lord fill my heart with love and keep me in the right way. I must read the Scriptures more. I need more faith.*

In the journal, Garfield's self-directed reproach was rooted in a need to appease his strict conscience. In the memory, his reproach of the sailors—expressed on behalf of himself—was rooted in a need to generate empathy for the well-being of people who like himself had been scorned and mistreated. Garfield's concern with betraying his moral and religious principles became a reality during a brief extramarital love affair he had with Lucia Calhoun in 1862. Upon finding out about the affair, his wife accused him of "lawless passion." He apologized for the affair and she forgave him. According to biographer Ira Rutkow:

> *Throughout his life, Garfield maintained intensely close relationships with a number of women ... Whether any of these associations included a sexual element remains historical conjecture.*

Driven by a mix of humiliation and powerlessness as exemplified in the memory, Garfield may have felt the need to compensate for his insecurity by "evening the score" and benefiting from the power and privilege of his position as a Congressman from Ohio. Serving in the House of Representatives from 1863-1880, he was involved in several incidents in which his integrity was questioned: In 1872 he was implicated in the Credit Mobilier scandal wherein he and several other congressman were accused of accepting bribes. Specifically, Garfield was charged with taking ten shares of Credit Mobilier stock and a loan of three hundred dollars in exchange for making sure that the business practices of the company were not questioned. Garfield denied any wrongdoing but was called before a congressional investigative committee. He testified that he was offered the right to purchase the stock but turned it down. He admitted accepting the loan but insisted that he repaid it in full and that the transaction in no way influenced his votes. According to biographer Ira Rutkow:

> *When the investigators delivered their report, they concluded that Garfield was guilty of accepting ten shares of stock, but that his interest in the company was minimal and it had not affected his congressional duties. Indeed, Garfield's real offense was that he knowingly denied to the House investigating committee that he had agreed to accept the stock and that he had also received a dividend of three hundred and twenty nine dollars.*

Two years later, in 1874, Garfield was involved in another scandal. As a practicing attorney in Washington D.C., he represented the

DeGolyer-McClelland Company in its bid for a contract with the District of Columbia to pave the dirt roads in Washington. Garfield received a fee of five thousand dollars for his legal services. Simultaneously, he was serving as chairman of the Committee on Appropriations in Congress and was responsible in part for the monetary affairs of the District. Garfield was indignant when his political opponents charged him with selling his influence in an apparent conflict of interest: "I propose to stand on my rights as an American citizen. There is nothing either of law or morals to prohibit a member of Congress from practicing his profession ... and this was as legitimate as any other practice."

After the scandal, Garfield returned to Ohio to fight for his reelection and defended himself against charges of corruption and dishonesty. In a letter he wrote to a friend, he described his current state of mind about the campaign: "I have had a hard and exhausting campaign but I shall beat the rascals who have been opposing me."

His state of mind during the campaign was reminiscent of his state of mind during the memory, that is, a determination to persevere despite receiving the harsh criticism from the old captain. Garfield won reelection handily in spite of the embarrassing scandal, receiving fifty-seven percent of the vote. After the victory Garfield described his feelings: "In view of the bitter and malignant assaults made upon me I feel that I came out better than could have been expected."

In the two scandals, Garfield's self-serving actions may have cancelled out underlying feelings that he was less worthy than his congressional peers. The urge to get ahead, impress others and see himself as a seasoned dealmaker may have compromised his actions. At best, the naïveté and poor judgment he demonstrated in both incidents left him vulnerable to the same type of harsh criticism that he faced in the memory.

Memory Two: "Bow Boy"

Humiliated by the razzing that Garfield suffered in Memory One, and not wanting to return home without adventure, money or pride,

Garfield decided he would pursue a more mundane job. He went to work for his cousin who owned a boat, the Evening Star, which traveled the waterways of the Pennsylvania and Ohio Canal. Garfield's job initially involved walking on a towpath next to the canal guiding the horses or mules that pulled the boat through the locks and the waterways. Subsequently, he was promoted to a "bower" which involved standing at the bow, the narrow front of the boat, while steering it through the canal. In the next memory, Garfield—who could not swim—grabbed for a rope hanging over the boat. Instead of holding, the rope began to unwind and he slipped off the wet deck and fell into the canal.

> *I felt I was coming to drowning. At length, however, the rope held and I was able to draw myself up until I could get a breath of air above the stagnant, stifling water… My feeble calls for help received no response from the sleeping people upon the boat. I at length made a great struggle and drew myself upon the boat. I was curious to know what had caused the rope to stop unwinding and carefully examining it, I found that just where it came over the edge of the boat it had been drawn into a crack and there knotted itself. I sat down in the cold of the night and in my wet clothes thought about the matter… I thought God had saved me for my mother and for something greater and better than canaling.*
> —*James Garfield, diary entry, Summer, 1848.*

The above incident marked the *fourteenth time* Garfield had fallen into the canal and survived. Nevertheless, he decided to continue his work on the canal. He commented in his journal, "My strong will had settled upon the life of a sailor and it would be difficult to break it."

The memory captured the difficult and dangerous circumstances that Garfield faced as he stood on the front of the bow. The memory challenged him to acknowledge his fear and uncertainty and to feel the strength of its implied message: "You can be successful if you just don't give up." It was from these dueling perspectives—hope and doubt, caution and adventure, strength and vulnerability—that he forged his identity. The memory helped him to recognize his ambivalence: one side planning to live a hard life and struggling to stay in the moment; the other planning to live a life of amazing adventure and opportunity.

Like a swimmer caught in different currents, Garfield-the-hard-worker felt the pull of reality and had difficulty seeing beyond the immediacy of his impoverished background. Garfield-the-swashbuckling-adventurer felt the pull of his dreams and hoped for glory and achievement. The memory highlighted the debate within himself between the importance of practicality and measured responses and the power of imagination and bold initiatives. The implication was that each side had its advantages and disadvantages and ultimately he would need to integrate them.

As a cautionary tale, the memory underscored life's difficulties and anticipated possible setbacks and dangers. What did Garfield learn from the memory? First, others should not underestimate his resolve and his determination to make something of himself. The second lesson was that even if he were able to overcome external dangers such as navigating the boat or falling into the water, he would still need to overcome his internal challenges. His sense of curiosity in the memory—wanting to know why the rope stopped unwinding when it did—represented his desire to untangle the knots or ambivalence within his own personality.

In a more indirect and light-hearted manner the memory suggested that some of the stress of standing on the bow resulted from his own fear and apprehension about drowning. For example, in 1881, President-elect Garfield was quoted in a Cleveland newspaper as saying, "I remember the old man who said he had a great many troubles in his life, but the worst of them never happened!"

In this statement, Garfield indirectly acknowledged the absurdity of trying to come to terms with life's troubles—troubles so anxiety provoking that they gave rise to mistaken if not distorted perceptions. The memory of the old man's comment helped him keep his worries and anxieties in perspective.

Born in the wilderness of Ohio, Garfield may have used the memory of near-drowning as a starting point for thinking through the limited opportunities available to him as an impoverished teenager. As he grew older, the memory may have motivated him to strengthen his resiliency. As he stated in his diary, "Poverty is very inconvenient but it is a fine spur to activity and may be made a rich blessing."

The memory implied that Garfield may have been born into poverty and a life of hard labor but it was not his destiny. He was determined to overcome any obstacle, such as falling into the canal, by demonstrating persistence, a strenuous work ethic and a readiness for any emergency. This attitude kept him feeling in "safe harbor." As Garfield once remarked, "My road must be through character to power." Each of the fourteen times he fell into the canal forced him to think of a better way to manage the present and shape the future. In short, the memory asked whether he could control the turbulent waters or whether they would control him.

It is truly amazing that Garfield would be a successful bow boy since he did not know how to swim; not one of the fourteen falls into the water caused him to "jump ship" and quit. The spirit of the memory is reflected in a contemporary song by John Legend (2014), *All of me*: "My head's underwater, but I'm breathing fine." The memory dramatized Garfield's wish to undertake a solitary journey, away from home to achieve a great accomplishment such as "beginning at the bottom of the business of sailing and carefully mastering it."

Over time, Garfield overcame many obstacles to become a teacher, minister, professor, university president, congressman, lawyer, senator and President of the United States. In a biography of Garfield entitled "From Canal Boy to President or the Boyhood and Manhood of James A. Garfield," no less than Horatio Alger cited him as a role model for aspiring youth wanting to make a difference in the world. The spirit of the memory offered an anchor of hope to the downtrodden. In part, the passion and drive that propelled his remarkable professional advancement was rooted in his impoverishment and in his fatherless background. In addition, his mother's personal influence and her association with the Disciples of Christ provided a moral context in which he developed a strong sense of duty and service to others.

Young James started school at the age of three, attending classes in a log hut. At ten years of age, he supplemented his widowed mother's income by working at home or on the farm of the neighbors. By the time he was fourteen, adventurous tales of the sea such as *Robinson Crusoe* thrilled and fascinated him. At the age of seventeen, Garfield started a journal in which he recorded that even upon thinking about sailing he would go "almost insane with the delight."

After about six weeks of working on the Pennsylvania and Ohio Canal, he was forced to return home to recover from an illness, apparently malaria. Upon recovering, his mother persuaded him to enter Geauga Academy, located in Chester, Ohio, where he became a skilled debater and worked as a carpenter, janitor, bellringer and part-time teacher.

At the age of eighteen, Garfield was baptized into the Disciples of Christ. According to his own account, his conversion occurred when he was "buried with Christ in baptism and arose to walk in newness of life." From 1851 to 1854, he studied at the Eclectic Institute in Hiram, Ohio, and earned his living as a school janitor. In 1854, he entered Williams College in western Massachusetts from which he graduated with the highest honors. He then returned to the Eclectic Institute as an instructor in Greek and Latin. In one possibly apocryphal story, Garfield was reported to have been able to simultaneously write Greek with one hand and Latin with the other.

During this period of time, he became a Disciples minister. Once, when he preached in Franklin, Ohio, he referred to his experience as a bow boy during his brief nautical career. He claimed it was evidence that: "The hand of the Lord has brought me thus far on the journey of life, and has preserved me for some wise purpose."

From 1857 to 1861, at the age of twenty-six, Garfield served as President of the Eclectic Institute (later named Hiram College). In 1858, he married Mary Lucretia Rudolph, a fellow classmate at Geauga Academy, with whom he had seven children. In 1859 he became the youngest member of the Ohio legislature. He embraced an anti-slavery stance, once writing in his diary, "*Servitium esto damnatum:* Slavery be damned." In 1861, studying law on his own he passed the Ohio bar. During the course of his legal career, he argued a number of cases before the Supreme Court of the United States. At the age of thirty, he became the youngest Union General in the Civil War.

The memory portrayed Garfield as hard-working, ambitious and self-reliant. Narrative details such as falling into the water served a significant purpose for him. It mattered less that he fell into the water so many times than that he was so resilient and supremely determined to escape death and return to the bow. It was not how many times he fell but that he recovered from each fall. In the face of all the trials he would endure in life, the memory presaged how he would defy the odds—death itself—and come back to accomplish great things.

As a young boy Garfield was known for being clumsy with an axe, wounding himself many times while chopping wood. Nevertheless, he did not give up. He would come back by taking jobs, as he noted in his journal, chopping wood for a month at fifty cents a day and cutting grass for fifty cents an acre. Furthermore, when he could no longer work on the canal boat because he was ill with what was called ague (malaria) he returned home to recover. Once again, he would prove his resilience—regaining his health after four months. He later wrote, "Only my powerful constitution could have saved me."

During the Civil War Garfield became so severely ill with dysentery that he was temporarily relieved of duty—returning to Ohio to regain his health. Just as he fell from the bow into the water, and somehow managed to survive, he recovered from his digestive illnesses and came back as Chief of Staff to General William Rosecrans.

At the Battle of Chickamauga, Garfield volunteered to take news of the Union defeat to General George H. Thomas. After a daring ride in which his horse was shot out from under him, he managed to complete the mission. The information he provided to General Thomas helped save the Army of the Cumberland from certain disaster. The same earnestness, determination and bravery that he showed as a bow boy also distinguished him at Chickamauga. As a result, he was promoted to Major General, the youngest officer to hold this rank.

In 1862, while still in uniform, Garfield was elected to the U.S. House of Representatives. Unsure if he should resign his active military commission as a General, he met with Abraham Lincoln to seek advice. Lincoln told him that he needed men with his military experience to serve in Congress in order to generate support for Republican causes in the House of Representatives. As a result, Garfield resigned his military commission and served as a congressman until 1880.

In a political context, Garfield's insecurities and his struggle to balance conflicting tendencies within himself frustrated both Democrats and Republicans. George Frisbie Hoar, a congressman who served with Garfield remarked:

> *Men who knew him very well say that when he led the House on the Republican side, and had led his party into a position which excited sharp conflict, they never could be sure that he would not get wrong at the last moment, or have some private understanding with the Democrats and leave his own party in the lurch. This was attributed to moral timidity.*

Another contemporary, John Sherman (the brother of General William Sherman) commented, "His will power was not equal to his personal magnetism. He easily changed his mind and honestly veered from one impulse to another."

Rutherford B. Hayes wrote that Garfield was a "Self-made man ... The truth is no man ever started so low that accomplished so much in all our history ... Yet, he could not face a frowning world."

These comments revealed Garfield's ambivalent nature and his tendency to vacillate, perhaps at times when he felt threatened or insecure. A need to balance different tendencies within himself may have predisposed him toward balancing divisions between Democrats and Republicans. In the process of examining the memory we gain a better sense of why he was internally directed toward a malleable posture.

In January 1880, Garfield was elected U.S. Senator from Ohio. Before his term as Senator began, he was nominated by the Republican Party—on the thirty-sixth ballot—to be their presidential candidate. He was sworn in as President in March, 1881. During the first week of his administration, when the new Postmaster General uncovered evidence of wrongdoing in the post office, Garfield ordered him to pursue the investigation, no matter where it led. Even when the investigation turned up evidence of bribery involving members of Garfield's own party, he told the Postmaster General, "Go ahead regardless of where or whom you hit. I direct you not only to probe this ulcer to the bottom, but to cut it out."

In this scandal—known as the Star Route Frauds—Garfield did not vacillate or show ambivalence. His decisiveness signaled to the nation that as President he would act in a more bold and aggressive manner, even if it meant alienating fellow Republicans. The government saved millions of dollars and Garfield's handling of the scandal set a heightened moral tone for conducting a responsible and ethical administration. His early actions as President foreshadowed that he would be motivated by his bold, innovative side as much as he would by the side that favored compromise and accommodation.

In July, 1881, barely 3 months into his administration, Garfield was shot by Charles Guiteau, a lawyer and ex-evangelist whose application to be ambassador to France was denied. He had repeatedly come to the White House demanding to be appointed as a reward for supporting Garfield's election. The assassination took place as Garfield was preparing an educational initiative to enable African-Americans to escape poverty—just as he had managed to escape from his own impoverished background. In the spirit of rising from poverty, his Inaugural Address emphasized the significance of an effective educational system in assuring a lasting solution to the problems faced by African-Americans.

After the assassination he lingered between life and death for more than ten weeks. In the end, he died from infections not caused by the bullet itself but by his doctors who did not accept the new theory of antisepsis advocated by British researcher Joseph Lister. They did not practice hand washing, surgical instrument cleaning or spraying the skin with antiseptic solution. Their probing of his wounds with their unwashed instruments and dirty fingers resulted in the one event from which he would not recover.

Using nautical imagery reminiscent of the memory, Garfield endured the ordeal of his assassination with his characteristic fortitude. Earlier in his life he had remarked:

> *I have sometimes thought that we cannot know any man thoroughly well while he is in perfect health. As the ebb-tide discloses the real lines of the shore and the bed of the sea, so feebleness, sickness and pain bring out the real character of a man.*

President Garfield died September 19, 1881 at the age of fifty.

Charles Guiteau was tried, sentenced to death, and hanged in 1882. Prior to the hanging he astutely declared that Garfield had died not from his bullet but from medical malpractice, arguing: "The doctors who mistreated him ought to bear the odium of his death, and not his assailant." Ironically, Guiteau was consumed by the same sense of resentment and victimization that Garfield experienced in Memory One. Resentment acted out with violence by Guiteau was only one of many possible responses to being victimized. Alternately, Garfield attempted to disavow his impulse for revenge and pursue a life in which he would seek justice and equity for others.

The assassination spurred his successor, Charles A. Arthur, into overhauling the patronage system that awarded plum positions to campaign supporters, as Guiteau had demanded. The result was the Pendleton Act of 1883 that insured that civil service appointments were based on competitive examinations as well as on talent and seniority rather than patronage.

Additionally, after Garfield's death the new theory of antiseptics gained general acceptance, forever transforming the field of medicine by the late 1880's.

Summary

The two memories occurred in the same relative time frame. The sense of humiliation and powerlessness in Memory One provided Garfield with the motivation to rise to the top; whereas the determination and resilience displayed in Memory Two provided him with the will to "stay the course." Together the memories reflected his internal contradictions and the factors that shaped them. Memory One was grounded in his self-identity as a self-conscious, marginalized adolescent. Memory Two no longer characterized him as a victim, but as a fully realized agent of his own destiny. In Memory Two he could literally and figuratively save himself and he had choices regarding the direction in which his life would go. He would not allow himself to drown in his disappointments; but he would challenge himself to be shaped by them.

Memory One carried a powerful message about how to live with resentments and grievances while fighting to break free of them. Memory Two implied a responsibility to discover one's own unique path and then to make the world a better and more equitable place. Both memories kept Garfield humble and self-effacing and laid the foundation for beliefs and attitudes that would influence him throughout his life: utilizing self-restraint rather than vindictiveness; showing compassion rather than revenge; and demonstrating resiliency rather than resignation.

As an adult Garfield referred to his childhood as that "strange, strange story, stranger to me than anyone else." Yet the two memories helped to clarify the "strange story" of his childhood by connecting his underdog, rags-to-riches and self-made image to an overarching concern with the plight of the poor and disenfranchised. Both memories represented a declaration of his reason to exist—to help make life better for other marginalized people, so they would have the opportunity to be recognized and valued as much as those who were born to wealth and privilege. To Garfield this declaration amounted to an ethical and religious imperative that he realized by becoming a politician. Both memories served to validate his role as a spokesperson for the poor and disenfranchised.

Upon Garfield's death, the words of Chauncey M. Depew, an attorney and U.S. Senator from New York, aptly reflected the essential themes of both memories such as overcoming adversity and the importance of hard-work, perseverance and self-reliance:

> *No boy in poverty, almost hopeless, thirsting for knowledge, meets an obstacle which Garfield did not experience and overcome. No youth despairing in darkness feels a gloom which he did not dispel. No young man filled with honorable ambition can encounter difficulty which he did not meet and surmount.*

Bibliography

Alger, Horatio From Canal Boy to President, or the Boyhood and Manhood of James A. Garfield. New York: John R. Anderson, 1881.

Brown, Harry and Williams, Frederick The Diary of James A. Garfield: Volume 1-4. Michigan State University Press, 1967.

Conwell, Russell H. The Life, Speeches and Public Services of James A. Garfield. Portland, Maine: Stinson and Company, 1881.

Degregorio, William The Complete Book of U.S. Presidents. Random House, 1984

Doenecke, Justus D. Presidencies of James A. Garfield and Chester A. Arthur. Lawrence: University of Kansas, 1981.

Millard, Candice Destiny of the Republic: A Tale of Madness, Medicine, and the Murder of a President. Doubleday, 2012.

A well-written and thought provoking book that includes a particularly interesting examination of the medical practices of the time.

Peskin, Allan   Garfield: A Biography. The Easton Press, Norwalk, Connecticut, 1978.
A comprehensive, well researched book containing over 600 pages. The book provides a balanced perspective on his life and contains useful and interesting insights into his personality.

Rutkow,Ira   James A. Garfield. Times Books, Henry Holt and Company, New York, 2006.
This book was written by a surgeon and historian and contains a concise description of Garfield's life. Moreover, the book contains an excellent analysis of the medical issues that were involved in his assassination, recovery and death.

Smith, Theodore C. The Life and Letters of James A. Garfield. Two Volumes. New Haven, 1925.

Thayer, William M. From Log Cabin to White House, Life of James A. Garfield. Boston: James H. Earle, 1881.

Chester A. Arthur

President of the United States,
1881-1885

Memory One: "The Gentleman Boss"

When Chester was a boy (age ten) you might see him in the village street after a [rain] shower, watching boys building a mud damn across the rivulet in the roadway. Pretty soon he would be ordering this one to bring stones, another sticks, and others sods and mud to finish the damn; and they would all do his bidding without question. But he took good care not to get any of the dirt on his hands.
— *Chester A. Arthur,* by George Frederick, page 7.

In the memory, in spite of humble origins, born in a log cabin, Chester A. Arthur set himself apart from other boys, foreshadowing the importance he would place on leading from behind the scenes. For future politician the memory represented the first time he viewed himself as a leader: knowing when to get involved, when to make things happen and when to keep his distance. The memory reveals some of the dynamics that were characteristic of his personality, such as a need to be in charge and to lead others. The detached leadership style he showed in the memory would later influence him as a teacher, principal, lawyer, Quartermaster General, head of the Customs House in New York, Vice President and President.

The perception of total control—"the boys did his bidding without question"—showcased him as a resourceful and capable leader who could take charge in an unexpected situation. Moreover, the memory provided him with a sense of confidence that after a rain shower occurred, he understood what was required and initiated a plan to solve the problem. The memory reinforced his belief that he could direct others to bring about social improvement in a way that transcended his own modest circumstances, such as being born in a log cabin. In his success as a ten-year-old who calmly handled a situation that was in need of organization, Arthur realized that being a leader was what he wanted to do for the rest of his life.

The public viewed Arthur as a "Gentleman"—someone who was congenial, approachable and distinguished; but he was also viewed as "the Boss"—someone with all the power to whom others deferred. This duality was reflected in the memory in which he was portrayed as a boss who directed the boys to finish the dam, and as a gentleman who made sure he did not get his hands dirty. Throughout his life, Arthur shifted between these two roles and the balancing act was given symbolic expression in the memory.

Manifestly the memory shows him as a leader; but it also reveals a latent characteristic of his personality, which was to be a follower. Did he identify with the boys in the memory who followed his orders? Or did he always see himself as someone who gave orders? As an adult with a position of authority would he be a confident leader poised to tell others what to do? Or would he be one of the boys and support the entrenched *status quo*? As we see in further examining the memory, he would move through life from one role to the other, reversing his position depending on the circumstances. In short, the memory showed him searching for his identity as a leader as he reconciled the conflicting demands of being both a gentleman and a boss.

Understanding the significance of this memory—and also Memory Two, which follows—requires a discussion in four areas: growing up in a religious home; as a teacher, principal and lawyer; as Quartermaster General and head of the Customs House in New York; and as Vice President and President. Arthur's leadership style would evolve during each of these phases based on the changing circumstances in which he found himself.

Growing up in a religious home

Chester A. Arthur was born in Vermont in a log cabin on October 5, 1829, the fifth of nine children and the first son of William and Malvina Arthur. William was born in Ireland and emigrated to Canada around 1818, before crossing the border into the United

States. William, a Baptist minister and staunch abolitionist, became an American citizen in 1843. According to biographer Greg Dehler:

> *The Canadian connection would follow Chester for the rest of his life. A scurrilous Democrat campaign book in 1880 asserted untruthfully that Chester Arthur had in fact been born in Canada and was not capable according to the constitution of becoming president.*

When Chester was born—presumably because he was the first son—a parishioner recalled that his father "danced up and down the room." As a child growing up, religious and ethical principles taught to him by his father helped to shape his beliefs, attitudes and actions. In 1835, his father helped to initiate the New York Anti-Slavery Society. According to biographer George Frederick Howe, Chester's father was:

> *Always vigorously partisan, never indifferent or neutral. His sharp tongue and conspicuous want of tact were consistently getting him into trouble and alienating his potential friends. Such misfortunes he no doubt set down as necessary evils for one who would preserve his independence. He was nothing if not independent!*

Contentious, opinionated and impatient with people who challenged him, the elder Arthur frequently quarreled with parishioners and trustees. As a result, the passionate curmudgeon was forced to leave several congregations and relocate his family. It is possible the father's fervent anti-slavery position was another factor that was responsible for the friction he encountered at the different parishes. The more his abolitionist views were attacked, the more pugnaciously he defended them and over time, he became increasingly alienated from his flock.

The family moved five times during Chester's first nine years, before they finally settled in Union Village, New York, in 1839. During this period of time, Chester was home-schooled by his father. While living in Union Village, Chester attended the local Academy for Boys. He was described by his principal as someone who was "frank and open in manners and genial in disposition." Unlike his father he did not pick fights and was even-tempered. He seemed more interested in activities such as hunting, fishing and camping with his friends than he was in attending religious services or adhering to religious orthodoxy.

Personality and lifestyle differences between father and son may have created tension in their relationship. From Chester's point of view, he was just a young boy craving fun and independence. Perhaps he was put off and disappointed by his father's rigidity and judgmental manner and his father was put off and disappointed by his son's lack of religious accountability and his easy-going persona. Chester may have viewed his father as a combative leader whose intemperate actions divided the parish and forced the family to relocate frequently. On the other hand—as evidenced in the memory—he viewed himself as a more restrained and poised leader whose actions united others for a common good.

They each played the role of a particular type of "boss" and carried themselves in different ways. Chester was the "good guy" who charmed people. His father was the moralistic preacher who put people in their place. As an adult, Arthur's affectionate nickname was the "Gentleman Boss" while his father was probably called something far less endearing. Yet, they both saw themselves as leaders who played a carefully crafted role in order to broaden their appeal and enhance their influence.

Given Chester's accommodating manner, the thought of disappointing or angering his cantankerous but devoted and loving father was too anxiety provoking. He may have felt that he needed to carry all of the hopes and wishes that his father missed out on during the years he moved from one parish to another. To avoid setting him off he may have deferred to his father's authority and tried to soothe or comfort him in order to win his support and approval. It must have been difficult to free himself from the demands of his strict conscience to be a loyal and dutiful son. In this light, his exacting conscience revealed itself in an anecdote from a friend who quoted him as an adult saying:

> *If I had misappropriated five cents, and on walking downtown saw two men talking on the street together, I would imagine they were talking of my dishonesty, and the very thought would drive me mad.*

As an adolescent, Chester tried to compensate for his unmet need for autonomy at home by becoming more demonstrative and occasionally non-compliant at school. For instance, in 1845, as a sophomore at Union College, a classmate remarked, "In disposition he was genial and very sociable, and he had a very good relative standing in his class though not a very diligent student."

Chester took part in a number of college pranks and was fined several times for skipping chapel, throwing the school bell in the Erie Canal and jumping on and off slow-moving trains. There was something about him—his good looks, his approachability, his leadership style—that registered with his peers. He had a knack for being agreeable and outgoing—not for being diligent. Perhaps that was the secret of his charming manner and what set him apart and ultimately alienated him from his parents. According to biographer Thomas Reeves:

> *Arthur and his brother William were both estranged from their parents to a degree because of their hostility to the faith ... Arthur never exhibited a personal commitment to the gospel of Christ that would have pleased his father.*

During the Civil War his mother wrote letters in which she communicated her husband's and her own consternation with their son's lack of faith:

> *Dear son, how long will you live in rebellion against God and refuse to obey his commandments? ... Oh that God would answer my prayer that before I am taken from life, you and Chester may come out publicly, confess Christ and be willing to be fools for his sake. I know he will lead you to everlasting life and glory, if you are willing.*

Over time, Arthur's need to be in control took the form of disengaging himself from his parents by not spending time with them. The distance Arthur had to travel to escape their influence, both geographically and in his lifestyle indicated how pressured he must have felt about his upbringing. According to biographer Greg Dehler:

> *The estrangement between William and his son over religion was a serious breech. In fact, Chet had a chilly relationship with both his parents after he moved to New York City (after the Civil War). He seemed to want desperately to leave the hardships of his youth behind, including his parents. On January 16, 1869 his mother Malvina died. William remarried, placing further distance between himself and his children. When his father was dying Chet came up from New York to see him, but did not stay long. William died on October 25, 1875, without his eldest son present.*

Even if their personalities and lifestyles were different, the political values his father taught him—as well as his Irish heritage—left a mark on Chester's inclinations and perspectives. For instance, in college he supported the Fenian Brotherhood, an Irish Republican organization founded in America. Moreover, his father was a Whig and in 1844, he supported former U.S. Senator and anti-slavery advocate Henry Clay for president.

Memory Two: "The Ash Pole"

[Chester] had taken an active interest in politics at a very early age. He sympathized with the Whig Party and was an ardent admirer of Henry Clay. It is related of him that during the contest between Polk and Clay, he was the leader of the boys of Whig parentage in Greenwich Village, who determined to raise an ash pole in honor of Henry Clay. They were attacked by the boys of Democratic parentage while doing so, and for a time driven off the village green. But they were rallied by young Arthur, and he leading a desperate charge, the Democrats were driven with broken heads from the field. Then, with a shout of triumph, the Whig boys raised the ash pole.

—The Republican Manual: History, Principles, Early Leaders, Achievements of the Republican Party. E. V. Smalley, p. 104

Following in his father's footsteps, Chester opposed James Polk—Clay's opponent; and—consistent with the dynamics recalled in Memory One—organized other students from his college to build an ash pole to honor and support the candidacy of Clay. They cut an ash tree and stripped off its branches. In turn, some of Polk's followers removed the ash pole, at which point Chester led the charge that resulted in a brawling fistfight. As an adult, Arthur later remarked, "I have been in many political battles since then, but none livelier, or that more thoroughly enlisted me."

In part the ash pole incident remained in Arthur's consciousness because he longed for his father's approval and politics represented the sustaining emotional link that bonded them together. In this regard, the image of an ash pole "propped up" their ambivalent relationship. In organizing both the building of the mud dam and the ash pole Chester viewed himself as the person in charge. However, in the ash pole incident the college student was learning that occasionally he would need to balance a top-down leadership style with a bottom-up effort to get his hands dirty—or in this case roughed-up. Some of his fellow students may have been threatened by his need to be in charge—others less so—but whatever they felt, Arthur would use his charm to put them at ease.

Perhaps Arthur was galvanized to win future political battles by summoning the memory of the ash pole—in which he both led from behind (organizing the activity) and from the front (brawling with adversaries). If he could do both, he would be a leader to be reckoned with! In short, the story of the ash pole highlighted Arthur's adventures and misadventures on the way to becoming a leader.

Teacher, Principal, Lawyer

After graduating from Union College, Arthur became a teacher. He taught at several different schools; and at one school in North Pownal, Vermont, future President James A. Garfield, the man who would choose Arthur as his Vice President, taught penmanship. In 1852, Arthur accepted the position of principal at the Choes Academy in Vermont where his sister was a teacher. His first test as a principal was to manage a group of recalcitrant boys who had overwhelmed several of his predecessors. Demonstrating the moderation of a gentleman-boss, he explained to the boys that he would deal fairly but firmly with their misbehavior. According to George Howe, "With considerable resourcefulness, Arthur eventually gained complete mastery of the entire department."

In addition, to deal with student misbehavior, Arthur initiated a behavioral intervention that involved sending an acting-out child to a primary classroom to sit with the younger students for a specified period of time. Arthur's career as a teacher and principal was short-lived as he wanted to pursue an alternative profession in which he would earn enough money to lead a more comfortable lifestyle. However, he actually left his mark as a supportive and caring educational leader whose actions may have influenced modern day techniques regarding behavioral intervention.

In 1854, after studying to become a lawyer and taking classes at a local academy, Arthur was admitted to the bar and moved to New York City. He took a position at the law office of Erastus D. Culver—an abolitionist lawyer and friend of his father—where he rose to become a partner. Arthur supported the same Whig philosophy and anti-slavery views that brought together his father and Mr. Culver. At this stage in his life, Arthur had learned the importance of deferring to those who had more experience and authority than he did. As a result, Mr. Culver trusted and depended on him to fulfill the objectives and overall mission of the firm.

Arthur assumed an influential role in two cases that addressed the issue of civil rights for African-Americans. In each case he argued for principles that were consistent with his father's abolitionist beliefs. The first case involved Jonathan Lemon, a slave owner who had brought eight slaves into New York from Virginia. Arthur's firm argued that slavery was illegal in New York so the slaves should be freed. Lemon argued that the slaves were not residents of New York and they were not bound by its laws. Through three trials and the

New York Court of Appeals, the courts decided in favor of Arthur's firm. The outbreak of the Civil War prevented the Lemon case from going to the Supreme Court. Arthur's specific legal responsibilities in this case are not known; however, he played an important role behind the scenes in prosecuting the case.

Arthur played a more direct role in a second case that involved an African-American schoolteacher, Elizabeth Jenkins. Jenkins was forcibly removed from a streetcar in New York and Arthur was responsible for taking her case to trial. The streetcar conductor maintained that Jenkins could not ride the car because it was full. Arthur argued that the teacher was removed because she was black. He won a judgment against the streetcar company for $250 plus court costs. As a result of this case, the New York City public transportation system was integrated.

In 1856 his legal mentor, Mr. Culver was promoted to a judgeship at which point Arthur started a new law partnership with Henry D. Gardiner. They both travelled to Kansas to purchase land and set up a law practice. At this time, Kansas was a battleground of pro- and anti-slavery forces that were divided over whether to allow or abolish slavery in the territories of Kansas and Nebraska. Arthur supported the anti-slavery position. His stay was cut short when he had to leave Kansas to support his fiancée, Ellen Herndon, whose father had died. Her father was a Commander in the United States Navy who went down with his ship when it sunk in a storm off Cape Hatteras, North Carolina, in 1857.

After helping her family resolve financial problems associated with her father's estate, Arthur moved back to New York and continued to practice law. In 1859 Arthur married Ellen Herndon who had been born and raised in a family of slaveholders from Virginia. Despite Arthur's anti-slavery convictions, the tactful and friendly lawyer found a way to get along with his wife's family—in spite of their opposing beliefs and attitudes.

In an effort to bolster his credentials as a leader, Arthur became involved in New York politics. At the time, the New York political scene was under the control of Thurlow Weed who was known as the "Dictator." Weed presided over a "spoils system" in which job seekers would be expected to give part of their salaries to him as payment for their employment. The system was referred to as "machine politics" and Arthur became "one of Weed's boys" who followed his orders. In his relationship with Mr. Weed, Arthur identified with the role of the boys in the memories who once followed his lead as he directed them to build the dam and later the ash pole.

 Quartermaster General and head of the Customs House in New York

At the recommendation of Thurlow Weed, Arthur was offered a patronage appointment on the staff of the Governor of New York, Edwin Morgan. The position, Engineer-in-Chief was of minor importance until the outbreak of the Civil War. At that point, Arthur was commissioned as a Brigadier General and assigned to the New York State Quartermaster Department. He was so efficient at housing, feeding and outfitting the troops that he was eventually promoted to Inspector General and then to Quartermaster General. In this capacity he developed cost-saving techniques to address the varied needs of the 100,000-plus men for which he was responsible. For instance, according to biographer Gregg Dehler:

> *He placed men in barracks instead of tents, to improve morale. He offset this cost by contracting directly with railroads for reduced rates for troop transportation instead of going through the war department.*

His behind-the-scenes maneuvering such as using private contractors and awarding contracts to the lowest bidder saved money for the war department and minimized bureaucratic problems. His innovative methodology such as "outsourcing" contracts would become commonplace more than a century later. Moreover, his eye for detail and meticulousness was recognized by his successor:

> *I found a well organized system of labor and accountability, for which the state is chiefly indebted to my predecessor, General Arthur, who, by his practical good sense and unremitting*

> *exertion, at a period when everything was in confusion,*
> *reduced the operation of the department to a matured plan, by*
> *which large amounts of money were saved to the government,*
> *and great economy of time secured in carrying out the details*
> *of the same.*

Since Arthur's position as Quartermaster General was a political appointment, he was relieved of his military duties in 1863 when a Democrat was elected as governor. As a result, he returned to being a lawyer in the firm of Arthur and Gardiner. His law practice flourished and he became a leading member of the social and financial elite. Through his association with Roscoe Conkling, the newly elected senator from New York, Arthur ascended in party politics, while at the same time helping Conkling establish one of the most powerful political machines in the country.

Arthur became chairman of the state Republican executive committee, and in 1871, he was named Collector of Customs for the Port of New York by President Ulysses S. Grant. The Custom House of New York was the largest in the nation and collected taxes on all goods that came into the port as well as fines for customs violations. The revenue—which represented 75% of the country's customs fees—was then transferred into the Federal treasury. Employing over one thousand people, the Customs House was the nation's largest federal employer.

In becoming "one of Conkling's boys" Arthur once again identified with the role of the boys in the memories. However, his elevated position of authority did not inspire him to use his power to advance necessary reforms at the Customs House. According to biographer George Howe, at this stage of Arthur's development as a leader:

> *Politics became a game for the promotion of a party to a*
> *position of control. He was not so much concerned with the use*
> *to which the control was put—so long as it was honest—as he*
> *was in getting and maintaining it.*

In his position as a collector of customs, Arthur staffed the Customs House with more employees than it needed and retained employees for their party affiliation rather than their merit as government officials. In the same way that New York columnist Jimmy Breslin once ridiculed Mayor Ed Koch in the 1970's-80's for "working incessantly at knowing nothing," Arthur maintained that he was unaware of any corruption taking place under his direction. He shared the sentiments of his boss and political mentor Conkling, who referred to civil service reform as "snivel service."

Although Arthur was not accused of personally profiting from his position, he did not oppose practices such as expecting federal employees to allocate a portion of their salary to support Conkling's campaign fund. Reminiscent of the memory, Arthur presented himself as a gentleman-boss whose job was to get things done—and to make sure that he did not get his own hands dirty. In short, the allure of being in charge was too enticing for him to oppose machine politics. During his first three years at the Customs House, Arthur's income came to more than $50,000 a year which included a percentage of the fines and penalties he collected. His salary was more than President Grant's and enough for him to enjoy the lavish lifestyle to which he became accustomed. According to biographer Kenneth D. Ackerman:

> *Arthur was the first president with his own valet, a man who could try on twenty pairs of pants before picking the right one and always ended up looking elegant and distinguished.*

Being a "fashion plate" with custom-tailored clothes gave him the advantage of distinguishing himself from the crowd (the boys) and projected an image that bolstered his self-worth and reinforced his credentials as a leader. The image of Arthur that comes to mind is the top-hatted fellow from the Monopoly board game who was originally known as "Rich Uncle Penny Bags." Some have speculated that this Monopoly figure was based on financier and banker J.P. Morgan, a contemporary of Arthur's and a "captain of industry" during his administration.

Arthur embraced the lifestyle of a quintessential big-city-machine politician. He delighted in entertaining leaders at elaborate dinners and elegant parties, enjoyed living in an expensive home and pursuing his favorite hobby, fishing. He was considered an expert angler once catching an 80-pound bass off the coast of Rhode Island. The cost was having a reputation for being a "Mr. Fancy Pants"— someone focused on style over substance. Another cost was neglect of his family as his wife sometimes resented the long hours he spent away from home. Arthur and his wife lost their son William at the age of three. Later they had two other children, Chester Allen, Jr. and Ellen. Biographer Thomas Reeves remarked, "The major obstacle to the happiness in the Arthur family was Chester's frequent absences."

In 1877 Republican Rutherford B. Hayes was elected President and he pledged to reform the civil service system. Hayes issued an order forbidding federal employees from "taking part in the management of political organizations, caucuses, conventions, or election campaigns." In addition, he appointed a commission to investigate corruption at the Customs House. As a result of the investigation he removed Arthur from his position for tolerating waste, enabling an inflated staff along with an excessive payroll and using government money to reward his political supporters.

To Hayes, Arthur was the epitome of unprincipled leadership, the triumph of political power in the service of self-serving goals. Hayes viewed him as a clever man and a canny operator who did what worked for Conkling and the "old boys' network," without any regard for the ethical or moral consequences. To Arthur, his role at the Customs House was to maintain the status quo—to be well-bred, well-connected and well-intentioned—rather than to actually stop or prevent corrupt or illegal practices. From his point of view, he was the person who soothed and placated Conkling—like he did his own father—but he did not change the essential nature of his partisan practices.

The more objective depiction may be that Arthur got caught up in what he thought was common and acceptable practice and he was either oblivious to or unconcerned with the moral and ethical consequences of his actions. Free of accountability from Conkling— or from some outside agency—he did what worked for "the machine," the Customs House and what advanced his own self-interests. What he experienced in his position was a combination of financial security and a sense of autonomy. This combination generated a sense of control—the need for which was first expressed in the memory.

Vice President and President

After being removed by Hayes from the Customs House, Arthur returned to his private law practice. At the same time, he served as president of New York's Republican Executive Committee and worked throughout the state on behalf of Republican candidates who supported Conkling. In 1880, Arthur's wife died suddenly of pneumonia at the age of forty-two, leaving him with the responsibility of raising a son and a young daughter. Away in Albany on business at the time, Arthur arrived home too late to say goodbye or to comfort and support his wife before she died. Typically, Arthur kept his emotional and private life walled-off behind layers of control; however, in this situation it was reported that he felt devastated and guilty for having been frequently absent from home. He remarked at the time, "Honors to me are not what they once were." Arthur never married again.

In 1880, when James A. Garfield won the Republican nomination for president, he realized that in order to win the national election he would need Conkling's support to obtain New York's electoral votes. As a result, Garfield offered the vice-presidential nomination to a Conkling supporter, Levi P. Morton. Morton turned down the nomination at the insistence of Conkling who was enraged that Garfield won the nomination over his preferred choice, former President Ulysses S. Grant. Moreover, Conkling believed that Garfield would lose the election to the Democrat, General Winfield Scott Hancock. Turned down by Morton, Garfield then offered the vice-presidency to Arthur.

Arthur accepted the nomination in part because it would provide him with national recognition and a forum to showcase his social prominence. In addition, he could remove the stigma of having been recently deposed from the Customs House by President Hayes. He wanted to eliminate the perception that he was another corrupt big city politician and as Vice President he would have an opportunity to redeem himself. The problem with redemption was that Conkling refused to buy it. When Arthur told him that he had been offered the vice presidency, Conkling remarked, "Well, sir, you should drop it as you would a red hot shoe from the forge." Arthur responded, "The office of the vice president is a greater honor than I ever dreamed of attaining. A barren nomination would be a great honor. In a calmer moment you will look at this differently." Conkling persisted, "if you wish for my favor and respect you will contemptuously decline it."

In a situation where he typically deferred to a dominating authority figure—as he had done with his father— Arthur found the fortitude to defy Conkling's wishes: "Senator Conkling, such an honor and opportunity comes to very few of the millions of Americans, and to that man but once. No man can refuse it, I will not. I shall accept the nomination and I shall carry with me the majority of the delegation."

In opposing him Arthur acted quickly and decisively, just as he did in the memory in the aftermath of the "shower." In part, the decision to accept the vice presidency was a way to preserve an image of himself as a resolute leader—an image that was given expression in both memories. Refusing to yield to Conkling was something of which he could be proud, as worthy of respect in its way as that of a ten-year-old leading the effort to build a dam for his community; or fighting to defend the monument (ash pole) that honored his political candidate.

During the presidential campaign, Arthur travelled throughout the state and spearheaded efforts to raise funds in order to secure the popular and electoral vote in New York. Garfield and Arthur carried New York by 20,000 votes and won nationwide by just 7,018 votes. After the election, the question of patronage became an issue that set the new Vice President against his President. In his capacity as a powerful senator and Arthur's mentor, Conkling still expected the vice president to do his bidding. He wanted him to persuade Garfield to find jobs for loyal Republicans in New York State. President Garfield refused to comply, at which point Arthur sided with Conkling over the President. Arthur's deference to his mentor was seen as a betrayal by Garfield. Apparently, he was still emotionally invested in being "one of the boys" and a key player within his powerful inner circle.

Less than four months into the Garfield administration, an assassin shot the president in the back and he died of complications two months later. After the assassination, Vice President Arthur received a letter from an American citizen named Julia Sand. She was a resident of New York City, and unknown to him. Subsequently, she wrote at least twenty-three other letters. What follows are excerpts from some of the letters she wrote:

August 27,1881:
The hours of Garfield's life are numbered—before this meets your eye, you may be President. The people are bowed in grief but—do you realize it?—not so much because Garfield is dying, as because you are his successor. What president ever entered office under circumstances so sad?

Great emergencies awaken generous traits which have lain dormant [sleeping] half a life. If there is a spark of true nobility in you, now is the occasion to let it shine... Faith in your better nature forces me to write to you—but not to beg you to resign. Do what is more difficult and more brave. Reform!

Once in a while there comes a crisis which renders miracles feasible. The great tidal wave of sorrow which has rolled over the country has swept you loose from your old moorings and set you on a mountaintop, alone.

Disappoint our fears. Force the nation to have faith in you. Show from the first that you have none but the purest of aims.

It is for you to choose whether your record shall be written in black or in gold. For the sake of your country, for your own sake and for the sakes of all who have ever loved you, let it be pure and bright.

September 25, 1881:
You are a better and nobler man, due to the manner in which you have borne yourself through this long, hard ordeal.

October, 1882:

> *Remember that you are President of the United States—work only for the good of the country. And bear in mind, that, in a free country, the only bulwark of power worth trusting, is the affection of the people.*

We can never know for certain the impact these letters had on Arthur. What we do know is that he directed most of his personal and official papers to be burned shortly before he died. The letters from Sand apparently had a profound effect on him because he preserved them in his files. Perhaps he kept the letters because—similar to the memories—they expressed confidence in his leadership and in his ability to rise to the challenge of the presidency. In this context, the letters can be viewed as yet another narrative that revealed his lifetime struggle to be a responsible and effective leader in the face of competing pressures. Moreover, similar to the memory, the letters urged him to take control of his life, overcome obstacles and think about how he could make a profound difference.

After the assassination, on September 20, 1881, Arthur took the oath of office in the living room of his New York home, remarking:

> *Men may die, but the fabrics of our free institutions remain unshaken. No higher or more assuring proof could exist of the strength and permanence of popular government than the fact that, though the chosen will of the people be struck down, his constitutional successor is peacefully installed without shock or strain … All the noble aspirations of my lamented predecessor… to correct abuses, to enforce economy, to advance prosperity, and to promote the general welfare … will be garnered in the hearts of the people, and it will be my earnest endeavor to profit, and to see that the nation shall profit, by his example and experience.*

With these words, Arthur reassured America that he would dutifully and faithfully serve them as their new President. Although the first memory had prepared him to assume an elevated leadership role it also posed the question of what type of leader he wanted to be?

Would he be a supplicant-in-chief (i.e. one of the boys) and defer to Conkling—or would he be a force for social good, as he was in both memories? His role as the consummate insider at the Customs House was well known. The challenge was to prove that he was no longer in the pocket of the establishment and that his decision-making would be guided by the needs of the American people rather than by his relationships with other insiders or machine politicians. One newspaper writer speculated:

> *Conkling had been in the habit of patronizing Mr. Arthur and had given him political orders for so many years that he could not imagine this pleasure-loving, easy-going man capable of rebellion.*

Many Americans thought Arthur was unfit to be president given his history as a machine politician and his removal from the Customs House. Others thought he was complicit in the assassination of Garfield, especially after newspapers quoted Garfield's assassin, Charles J. Guiteau as saying, "I am a Stalwart, and Arthur will be President." (Republicans who supported Conkling were called Stalwarts). Despite these misgivings, Arthur rose to the occasion and assumed the role of an independent and challenging leader. In effect, the comments he made when he took the oath of office represented his own personal Declaration of Independence.

Arthur refused to offer Conkling the position he sought as Secretary of State and did not follow his advice regarding who should be removed and appointed to the Cabinet. On one occasion, when Arthur held his ground, an observer noted, "Conkling left the room, swearing that all of his friends had turned traitor to him." Perhaps one factor responsible for the eventual breakup of Arthur's relationship with Conkling was the suspicion that Conkling would be perceived as the man-behind-the-scenes rather than Arthur himself—the driving force behind the building of the dam and erecting of the ash pole. As he did with his father, Arthur distanced himself from Conkling rather than continue to interact with him and be viewed as a puppet—or be reminded of his own feelings of dependency.

The message to Conkling and the world was clear: Arthur was now the confident, take-charge leader he perceived himself to be in the memories. Just as President Ronald Reagan remarked in 1984, "America is back, standing tall," so, too, was Chester A. Arthur. Subsequently, in order to soothe his hurt feelings, Arthur offered Conkling a seat on the Supreme Court; but the message of who was in charge had been received and he refused the offer. Like he had been with his father, Arthur remained estranged from Conkling for the rest of his life.

Convinced that his background at the Customs House could help at a time when the public was ready for reform, Arthur assumed the role of a challenging and shrewd leader. One party leader noted, "He isn't Chet Arthur anymore; he's the President." He supported a bill called the Pendleton Act which created the Civil Service Commission. The commission sought to develop performance standards; recognize employees for good work rather than party affiliation and make it illegal for political parties to take money from government employees. The former champion of the spoils system and head of the Customs House—a top-down command-and-control organization—was now responsible for revamping the civil service system and making it more open and responsive to its employees.

Arthur pursued and completed an investigation of corruption within the U.S. Postal Service that had begun during the Hayes' administration. He boldly vetoed nineteen million dollars for "pork barrel" legislation involving infrastructure improvements throughout the country, known as the Rivers and Harbors Act. In doing so, he alienated powerful congressmen by objecting to provisions that were intended only to benefit their districts and line their pockets. He battled with Congress to provide funding to rebuild and modernize the U.S. Navy which was unprepared at the time to protect the nation in case of war. He supported the Navy Bill which was designed to construct new steel ships and created the Naval War College in Rhode Island and the Office of Naval Intelligence.

Arthur also disagreed with Congress on the Chinese Exclusion Act. This bill was intended to keep Chinese people from immigrating into the United States for twenty years and would have denied citizenship to U.S. residents of Chinese ancestry. Arthur threatened to veto the bill because he believed it compromised their civil rights and finally worked out a compromise with Congress that limited Chinese immigration for ten years instead of twenty. He advocated for the civil rights of Native Americans by protecting their land from encroachment by settlers and promoting funding for their education, especially vocational instruction. Lastly, in the wake of a Supreme Court decision that declared the Civil Rights Act of 1875 unconstitutional, and took away African-Americans' equal rights in public accommodation, Arthur proposed legislation to counteract the negative impact of the Court's decision.

Arthur's reform agenda was a worthy reminder of memories in which he used his leadership skills to benefit the community as a "bossy" but well-intentioned young man who aspired to lead. As President he could look back at the memories to measure the extent to which he had achieved his goal of becoming an effective leader. When Arthur refused a political favor to a New York Republican, he remarked, "If you were still president of the New York County Republican Committee, you would be here right now asking for this very thing." "I certainly would," Arthur responded, "but since I came here I have learned that Chester A. Arthur is one man and the President of the United States is another." In both the aftermath of the assassination of Garfield and the "shower" in the first memory, he had demonstrated his ability to be a force for social good.

As President, Arthur successfully steered a course between being a hospitable gentleman and a boss. In his role as a gentleman he hired Louis C. Tiffany to redecorate the White House and he included such modern innovations as an elevator and indoor plumbing. The presidential carriage was both stylish and conspicuous in its appointments of leather, lace and the president's monogram. The harness was mounted with silver and was drawn by two matched mahogany-colored horses. The *New York Times* said the carriage was "the finest which has ever appeared in the streets of the Capital." Arthur fulfilled his social obligations by hosting lavish gatherings with multi-course dinners that were prepared by his personally chosen French chef. He wore tuxedos to dinner and guests stayed until after midnight, drinking fine wines and consuming rich foods.

Indulgent eating habits and failure to exercise did not help Arthur's health and during his term in office he suffered from a kidney disease that slowly depleted his strength. In an effort to preserve his image of himself as a strong and vibrant leader he did not disclose this illness—Bright's disease, or nephritis—to the public. Although he thought about running for a second term he decided not to, as he told his son, because he did not feel well enough to handle the duties of the presidency for four more years. At the end of his term in 1885, he returned to New York; and in 1886 he died of Bright's disease. According to biographer Kenneth D. Ackerman:

> *Among the thousands of celebrities who attended his funeral service in New York City, Arthur would have appreciated the lone figure of Roscoe Conkling, keeping to himself in a side pew, grieving quietly for his old friend with whom he hadn't spoken in years.*

Summary

The two memories captured the spirit of leadership that empowered the "Gentleman Boss" throughout his life. Arthur perceived himself as a natural leader who had the ability to overcome and find solutions to events over which he had no control such as the shower of his youth and the opposition forces to the ash pole. He was a problem-solver who had the confidence to handle difficult situations, and—unlike his father—the charm to arouse good will in his followers rather than resentment. His decisive actions in the memory reminded him that in a crisis the boys believed in him. They believed in him because he did not get rattled; he maintained control over himself; and by keeping his hands clean, his presentation was—literally and figuratively—immaculate.

Similarly, in the aftermath of the assassination of Garfield, Arthur dispelled the American peoples' initial skepticism. They believed in Arthur, in his resolve to overcome his negative reputation, in his commitment to pursue legislation that challenged the interests of his own party and in his quest to be a steward for the best interests of the American people. Just as he won the respect of his peers in the memories, as President he won the respect of the American people. Mark Twain commented:

> *I am but one in 55 million; still, in the opinion of this one-fifty-five-millionth of the country's population, it would be hard to better President Arthur's administration. But don't decide till you hear from the rest.*

Biographer Zachary Karabell remarked,

> *Arthur adopted a code for his own political behavior but subject to three restraints; he remained to everyone a man of his word; he kept scrupulously free from corrupt graft; he maintained a personal dignity, affable and genial though he might be. These restraints ... distinguished him sharply from the stereotype politician.*

Publisher Alexander K. McClure explained Arthur's presidential leadership in the following way:

> *No man ever entered the presidency so profoundly and widely distrusted, and no one ever retired ... more generally respected.*

Memories from his youth that accompanied Arthur throughout his life acquired special meaning when he reached the zenith of his power. In his role as President, the memories helped him to renew the conviction and confidence on which he first based his desire to be a leader. In part the memories were instructive for the dichotomies they established: the difference between his leadership style and his father's; the difference between being a leader and being one of the boys; and the difference between being a boss and a gentleman. Depending on the circumstances, the memories provided valuable clues regarding which role he should or would assume.

During childhood Arthur chose between accommodating his father's combative temperament and expressing his own need for autonomy. During his marriage he chose between attending to the needs of his family and engaging in the time-consuming social scene which was requied. At the Customs House he chose between living the powerful life of a self-serving big city boss and reforming an organization where deception and graft were the orders of the day. At the White House he chose between being his own person and subordinating himself to partisan politics.

Throughout his career, Arthur was known as a machine politician but he also had an independent streak and he defied easy categorization from those who sought to define him as either a social dandy or a political hack. His own Republican party expected him to be one of the boys and perform the toadying role to which they had become accustomed. In a famous quote, F. Scott Fitzgerald once said there are "no second acts in American lives." However, drawing upon the memories to guide, shape and inform his decisions, Arthur successfully recast himself from the supporting role of a malleable machine politician to the leading role of a principled and forward-thinking President. In the latter role, he was center stage challenging other politicians—even from his own party—and working on behalf of the best interests of the United States.

Bibliography

Ackerman, Kenneth. Dark Horse: The Surprise Election and Political Murder of President James A. Garfield. Carrol and Graf Publishers: New York, 2003.

Doenecke, Justus. The Presidencies of James A. Garfield and Chester A. Arthur. Lawrence: University Press of Kansas, 1981.

Feldman, Ruth. Chester A. Arthur. Twenty-First Century Books: Minneapolis, 2007

Howe, George. Chester A. Arthur: A Quarter-Century of Machine Politics. New York: Frederick Ungar Publishing Company,1935.

Karabell, Zachary. Chester Alan Arthur. The American Presidents Series: New York Times Books, 2004.
> *A brief but concise and compelling portrayal of Arthur's life. The epilogue is a particularly insightful summation of Arthur's impact and accomplishments.*

Reeves, Thomas. Gentlemen Boss: The Life and Times of Chester Alan Arthur. Newton, Connecticut: American Political Biography Press, 1998.
> *A thorough and methodical examination of Arthur's life. This book is a valuable source for those seeking the details of machine politics and other specific aspects of Arthur's career.*

Smalley, Eugene Virgil. The Republican Manual: History, Principles, Early Leaders, Achievements of the Republican Party: with Biographical Sketches of James A. Garfield and Chester A. Arthur. American Book Exchange, 1880.

Benjamin Harrison

President of the United States,
1889-1893

Memory One: "Mother's Prayer"

Benjamin Harrison was raised in a home in which his father and mother had a strong allegiance to the Presbyterian faith. The family attended a local Presbyterian church every Sunday. Daily prayer and Bible reading nurtured conviction between Sundays, which generally saw the family headed some distance to church. When bad weather prevented the trip, they still kept the Sabbath conscientiously, shunning worldly activity, the better to contemplate the gift of God's grace. Later in life, Harrison remembered the awe he felt at the nightly ritual of his mother withdrawing from the family circle to commune alone with her heavenly Father. She bore as much solicitude for children's souls as for her own; she once wrote the teenaged Benjamin, "I pray for you daily that you may be kept from sinning and straying from the paths of duty." As a grown man of faith and responsibility, he made this prayer his own.

—*Benjamin Harrison*, by Charles W. Calhoun, page 10

In a campaign biography by General Lew Wallace—the author of *Ben Hur* and lifetime friend of Benjamin Harrison—the memory was described as "one of Benjamin's earliest recollections, that to which at this late date he refers with profoundest reverence of feeling." In the memory a young boy saw his mother giving him a lasting legacy—that is, showing by example the importance of introspection and prayer in order to reflect on one's responsibilities and duties. A memory of his mother's daily prayer: "May God bless you and keep you continually under His protecting care," was a way of calling attention to something inside of him that was longing for inner peace, solitary reflection and spiritual guidance.

At the time of the memory, Harrison's identity was evolving, and he projected different parts of it onto his mother. Her preference for solitary reflection and piety nurtured a desire in Harrison to emulate that. At the same time, his mother's actions represented his own inclination for internal conversations about responsibility and duty. As an adult, reciting the prayer helped him to be more like the idealized view he had of his mother. The memory was a testament to her steadfast love and determination to protect him.

Simultaneously the memory offered a rationale for understanding the foundations of Harrison's inner-directed, reserved personality, and it also shaped how others responded to him. It revealed a preference for privacy rather than sociability that often kept others from feeling as if they knew him. The problem with the memory was that it implied he could go it alone, that he could rely on himself and his own thoughts and could not always rely on others. Harrison's tendency to withdraw into himself was at the root of his difficulty in projecting warmth, and contributed to the oft-stated description of him—even by his own staff—as the "Human Iceberg."

The life of Benjamin Harrison is the story of a thoughtful, self-reflective thinker whose earliest memory set the stage for his notable achievements as a lawyer, soldier, general, senator and president. His memorial proclaimed that Harrison "represented what is best in public and private life."

Benjamin Harrison was born on a farm adjacent to his grandfather's estate August 20,1833, in North Bend, Ohio. He was the namesake of his great-grandfather, Benjamin Harrison, who was a Revolutionary War hero, Governor of Virginia, signer of the Declaration of Independence and contributor to the Constitution. His grandfather, William Henry ("Old Tippecanoe") was a general, first Governor of the Indiana territory, congressman, senator and ninth President of the United States. His father, John Scott Harrison, was a farmer and two-term U. S. congressman from Ohio. As a farmer, Benjamin's father struggled to meet his financial obligations due to problems he experienced both in farming and purchasing risky property. As a politician, he served as a Whig in the House of Representatives and supported compromise legislation designed to avoid the dissolution of the Union such as the Kansas-Nebraska Bill. Benjamin's mother, Elizabeth Irwin Harrison, was descended from Scottish immigrants and was brought up strictly observing the principles of the Presbyterian faith.

John and Elizabeth raised nine children—Benjamin being their second-born—in a small frontier farmhouse by the Ohio River. Benjamin was a restless and driven child who grew up immersed in a family heritage dedicated to public service with a strong belief in religion and prayer. He enjoyed swimming, hunting and fishing; and his responsibilities included feeding the cattle, hauling wood and milking cows.

Memory Two: "The Grandson of Nobody"

Although he was cognizant of the fact that he needed to live up to the expectations of his illustrious family, he also felt the need to prove himself worthy by demonstrating his merit rather than capitalizing on his family name. This dynamic was revealed in an incident that occurred in 1856 that involved the initial development of the Republican Party. According to biographer Harry J. Sievers:

> *The leaders found themselves desperately in need of speakers whose name might command respect and whose presence would serve to whip up some enthusiasm. Harrison was quietly at work in his (law) office when a number of gentlemen came in and insisted that he make a speech to a political gathering in the street outside. Harrison protested, as he did on a number of other occasions, his lack of preparation. These men, however, we are in no mood to be denied. They picked up his five-foot-seven frame and carried him downstairs, never permitting his feet to touch the ground until they had placed him on a store box that had been set up in the street. At once he was introduced as the grandson of ex-President William Henry Harrison. Flustered and a bit nervous, the young speaker momentarily crossed up the political leaders by refusing to draw on the political capital of his grandfather. With an air of youthful defiance he said, "I want it understood that I am the grandson of nobody. I believe that every man should stand on his own merits."*

Memories are often stories we tell ourselves about what we would like to become. When Harrison told the crowd, "I am the grandson of nobody," he expressed the wish to be viewed as his own man and not rest on the laurels of his family name. He was the Harrison who would prove that his accomplishments were the consequences of merit rather than privilege. The underlying message in Harrison's statement was once expressed by Rabbi Zusya (1718–1800), who said, "In the world to come they will not ask 'Why were you not Moses' but 'Why were you not yourself?'"

The first memory, of his prayerful mother, motivated Harrison to emulate her example; in the second memory, his pronouncement of being "grandson of nobody" expressed his desire to be his own man. The two narratives illustrated the chasm between a conforming and non-conforming person. The thread connecting them was the importance Harrison placed on being his own person. In each situation he formulated a different aspect of his personality: in one he projected a person deep in thought; in the other he was a self-sufficient figure who would one day prove himself on a national and world stage. The two inner voices were each to some degree capable and incapable of understanding the other.

Professing himself as "the grandson of nobody" was inspirational because it revealed his desire to eliminate an image of himself as "just another privileged Harrison." In this sense, the memory may have symbolized the first time he tried to free himself from the "burden" of his family name. Then again, the image of being carried off against his will confronted Harrison with his vulnerability. He offset his anxiety about the latter with a comment that not only disavowed his heritage but could be perceived as iconoclastic. In this sense, the episode foreshadowed a tendency—in social encounters—for him to say or do something that suggested an idiosyncratic manner. This is illustrated in his childhood and early education.

Young Benjamin began his education in a log cabin schoolhouse built by the Harrison family. Other students at the school included his brothers and sisters and the children of other farmers. One teacher hired by the family described him as the "brightest of the family, but he was terribly stubborn about many things. He would insist on having his own way not only with me, but with his mother."

Harrison excelled in reading and writing. His passion for spending hours reading books was nurtured by a preference for being alone—as was presaged in the first memory—and the large number of books that were available in his grandfather's library. At his mother's request he avidly read Bunyan's *Pilgrim's Progress*. Perhaps in reading this allegorical book in which the protagonist is weighed down by the burden of knowledge of his sin, he was reminded of his own burden—as suggested in the second memory—in carrying the weighty expectations of his family name.

The origins of Benjamin's insular and somewhat out-of-touch social presentation was demonstrated in an episode he had with his grandfather, just before he left for the White House for his grandfather's inauguration in 1841:

> *The eight-year-old could not resist the temptation presented by a stand highly piled with red-cheeked apples, and so began to fill his pockets just as he was wont to do under the favorite trees of his father's orchard. Of course, there was no resistance to this till the apple-woman saw him walk innocently and unconcernedly away. Her shrieks called the attention of the grandfather to the comical situation and the account was readily adjusted.*

This situation may have been "comical" to the grandfather, but it reveals the extent to which this very bright eight-year-old was oblivious to acceptable social behavior.

At the age of fourteen, in order to prepare Benjamin for college, his father arranged for him to leave home and attend a rigorous, all-boys high school academy in Cincinnati. He was expected to spend long hours studying. One of his favorite teachers, a Professor Bishop, impressed him with the following advice: "Education is getting possession of your mind, so you can use the facts as the good mechanic uses his tools." The professor's memorable words served to reinforce the thoughtful and inward-looking thinking style that was inspired by Memory One.

Harrison was an excellent student whose academic success qualified him to bypass his first two years of university studies. Even if Harrison "used the facts as the good mechanic uses his tools," he seemed to lack a charming or graceful social manner. Raised in an atmosphere in which he expected nothing short of perfection from himself, he had a tendency to be apprehensive or uptight when he was exposed to new or spontaneous social encounters. In such situations, he appeared to be overly vigilant and rigid, as if bracing himself for the worst. As one friend described him,

> *He was a quiet, undemonstrative man, and was credited with being cold and unsympathetic by those who saw him only in his public capacity, and when acting under the stress and strain of public duty.*

During his stay at the academy, Harrison became friendly with Caroline Scott, the daughter of one of his teachers, and his future wife. Her lively and outgoing personality stood in contrast to his reserved and modest manner. Harrison's father wanted him to attend a prestigious university such as Harvard or Yale. However, financial difficulties necessitated Benjamin's enrollment at Miami University in Oxford, Ohio. The summer before he was scheduled to start college his mother died in childbirth.

From this point forward, the first memory was a comforting reinforcement of his special relationship with his mother; and how she provided him with a caring but distant model of relating to others that he emulated in his own social interactions. In this light, the memory is a reflection on the meaning of her pivotal death in his life. Recalling the memory helped him to better understand the significance of what her presence had meant to him.

At Miami University he joined the local Presbyterian church and, like his mother, became a lifelong Presbyterian who regularly attended services. He was known as a smart, stern and religious student who did not spend much time with his classmates. He was the adult in the room at all times. He impressed his classmates with his public speaking skills. He became president of the Union Literary Society, a debating club that contained its own well-stocked library. In 1852, at the age of nineteen, Harrison graduated with Honors and ranked fourth in his class.

Early Law and Political Career

Although Harrison's father wanted him to become a Presbyterian minister, a number of factors influenced his decision to become a lawyer: his sense of independence, his legalistic thinking style, and a memory of his recently deceased mother who had shaped his principled conscience. In 1853, at the age of twenty, he married Caroline Scott ("Carrie"), and went on to study for the bar while working as an apprentice at a Cincinnati law office. After passing the Ohio bar exam in 1854, Harrison and Carrie moved to Indianapolis, Indiana, to practice law. In part, their decision to move to Indiana was influenced by his need to be his own person and to establish his own identity, as indicated in Memory Two.

> *I long to cut my leading strings and acquire an identity of my own. Were I to continue on here [Ohio] it would be long ere that people should cease to regard me as a boy, and almost as long ere I should cease to regard myself as such.*

In their new home, Carrie loved entertaining and celebrating holidays. She enjoyed painting and was an accomplished musician with an artistic temperament. On the other hand, Harrison had an introverted temperament but he enjoyed spending time with his wife and their two children, Russell and Mary. He found in his wife someone who could bring out qualities in him that were missing in the first memory.

When Supreme Court Justice Oliver Wendell Holmes met President Franklin Roosevelt in 1933, Holmes opined that Roosevelt had a "second-class intellect but a first-class temperament." Conversely, it could be said that Harrison's overall profile was the opposite of Holmes' description of Roosevelt: "a first-class intellect but a second-class temperament." One of the challenges facing Harrison would be applying his first-class intellect to meet the complex social demands expected not only of a successful lawyer but of someone born into a famous family.

In 1856, as a young lawyer, Harrison supported the Republican Party's first presidential candidate, General John C. Fremont. In 1857, he entered politics himself and won election as Indianapolis City Attorney. Following that, he served as secretary of the Republican State Central Committee; and in 1860 he campaigned for the presidential candidate, Abraham Lincoln. Determined to fulfill the Harrison family destiny in his own right, the ambitious and hard-working lawyer/politician took on the challenge—in addition to his full-time law practice—of running for office as the Republican candidate for Indiana Supreme Court Reporter. He won the election and in that capacity he summarized all the Court's trials and decisions and then published them in book form.

Harrison's tendency to over-extend himself concerned his friends as well as his family. His driven and restless nature created a tense atmosphere in which he could be viewed as a difficult person with whom to work. One friend warned him, "You will most certainly result dangerously, if you continue your present mode of life." In addition, his father wrote a letter in which he pleaded with him to "not overtax yourself ... for what is wealth and honor without health?... too much care and study is apt to make a man unsocial and morose."

According to biographer Harry Sievers, as a Supreme Court Reporter, Harrison "hated stupidity, expecting of subordinates the same high level of workmanship of which he himself was capable." In one incident, a typesetter in the Supreme Court book room reported:

> *Without a word or sign of recognition the paper was almost jerked from your hand when you presented it to him and asked what a certain word was. If he had no trouble in deciphering it, you were told in a harsh, unpleasant voice what it was, but if he had trouble in making it out, it seemed to anger him.*

Impatient to meet his own exacting standards, Harrison could become peevish at the mere thought of his own imperfection. In the process of proving himself he unintentionally alienated others. Despite his impatience and irritable temperament, Harrison developed a reputation for being a devout and exemplary Presbyterian—like his mother in the memory. The church elders remarked:

> *He became a teacher in the Sabbath school, he was constant in his attendance on church services; his voice was heard in prayer meetings; he labored for and with young men, especially in the YMCA. And in whatever way opened, whether public or private, he gave testimony for his faith and the lordship of his master.*

In his law practice, Harrison developed a reputation for being a sober, principled lawyer who painstakingly followed the facts. He was the archetype of the resolute lawyer, well prepared and ready for courtroom battle. In one case, he assisted in the prosecution of a hotel servant charged with poisoning a guest's coffee. In preparation for the trial, he exhaustively researched the chemistry of poisons in the human body. He was highly praised for his expertise and thoroughness in questioning the physicians who testified in the case. Biographer Lew Wallace described him:

> *He is characteristically straightforward, and his comparisons are never far fetched; his figures of speech are always closed in the simplest words, so that he is entertaining to everybody who hears him, and easily understood by everybody. The secret of his power, whether in court or on the stump, lies in the fact that he never fails to make himself perfectly understood.*

Soldier and General

In 1862 President Abraham Lincoln asked for an additional three hundred thousand men to volunteer as soldiers for the Union Army. The governor of Indiana pledged to help and asked for Harrison's assistance to create a new military regiment called the Seventieth Indiana Volunteer Regiment. The governor hoped to convince people to volunteer by capitalizing on the Harrison family name, and his reputation as a successful lawyer. To this end, he was commissioned as an officer, with the rank of second lieutenant. Within a short period of time he was successful in recruiting almost one thousand men and was promoted to the rank of colonel and appointed the regiment's commander.

What could Harrison's memories teach him about how to be a strategic military thinker who could assess an unfamiliar situation and then develop and execute a plan? Perhaps they taught him to retreat to the privacy of his own thoughts and use his first-class thinking skills without relying on his illustrious name. For example, away at war he used the self-reflection and the self-reliance that the memories foreshadowed in a letter he wrote to his wife:

> *I have talked enough about myself and my humble military career. Lest your affection might lend you to exaggerate my merits as a soldier, let me assure you that I am not a Julius Caesar or Napoleon. I am but a plain Hoosier Col., with no more relish for a fight than for a good breakfast.*

But how do you show someone whose early memories provided him with good reason to withdraw into his own thoughts that it was also important to reach outside of himself and serve his country in wartime? Perhaps it was unnecessary to show him because the memories called attention both to his religious responsibilities as a devout Presbyterian; and one who needed to excel under his own volition. On one occasion before entering the battlefield he wrote to his wife:

> *Pray to God—1st That he will enable me to bear myself as a good soldier of Jesus Christ. 2nd That he will give me valor and skill to conduct myself so as to honor my country and my friends and lastly that if consistent with his holy will, I may be brought "home again" to the dear loved ones.*

According to biographer Charles Calhoun, General Harrison:

> *... held religious services and "family prayers" in camp, tried to enforce some semblance of repose on the Sabbath, read religious tracts to men in the camp hospital, and otherwise sought to promote a sense of Christian patriotism.*

In doing this, Harrison seemed to be replicating in the camp what happened in Memory One—that is, a religious and family atmosphere in which daily services and prayers are held in order "to contemplate the gift of God's grace." Both memories inspired Harrison to set aside a contemplative space where he could aspire to be himself—an original—rather than a copy of his famous war-hero grandfather who successfully fought battles with Native Americans and during the War of 1812.

Some soldiers thought Harrison's disciplined, exacting manner was harsh and oppressive. However, his reputation for being a "chilly" commander coexisted with a heated commitment to preparing for battle—studying and reading books about war tactics for hours at night—and a fiery sense of patriotism and courage. Overall, Harrison earned the trust and confidence of his regiment and—given his five-foot-seven frame—was nicknamed "Little Ben." One soldier remarked that the men were "glad to fight by the side of Little Ben, who shirked nothing, and took just the same chance of getting a bullet through the heart as we did."

Harrison developed his stellar military reputation under General William Tecumseh Sherman in Georgia in 1864. In the Atlanta campaign, he would fight more battles than his grandfather fought in his entire military career. In one battle at Peach Tree Creek, "Little Ben" and his men met hard-charging Confederate soldiers in hand-to-hand fighting, and with him leading the charge they successfully forced them to retreat. After the battle his commanding officer, General Joseph "Fighting Joe" Hooker was so impressed that he told him, "By God Harrison, I'll make you a Brigadier General for this fight." Subsequently, President Lincoln nominated Harrison to the rank of Brigadier General, and praised his "manifest energy and gallantry."

In the battle at Peach Tree Creek, Harrison demonstrated outstanding merit and, at the same time fulfilled his lifetime desire to pursue something noble and to live up to the expectations of the family name, while making it his own. In a letter to his wife he remarked, "The family's famous name is as safe in my keeping as in that of any who now bear the name. We must not however think too much of the praises of the newspapers, nor forget that to God who sustains me belongs all the honor."

Post-War Veteran

At the end of the war Harrison went back to Indianapolis to rebuild his reputation as one of the state's leading lawyers and resume his position as a court reporter. In 1868 President Grant appointed Harrison to represent the federal government in a civil suit filed by Lambdin P. Milligan, whose controversial wartime conviction for treason led to the landmark U.S. Supreme Court case known as *ex parte Milligan*. During the Civil War, Milligan—an Indiana lawyer—opposed President Lincoln's policy of drafting men into the Union army. When he gave a speech in Fort Wayne, Indiana, he argued that civilians should resist the draft and, as a result, he was arrested, imprisoned and sentenced to death for being a traitor.

In 1866 the U.S. Supreme Court reversed the death sentence, freed Milligan and ruled that the army had no right to arrest and try a civilian where there were adequate civilian courts. Milligan then sued the U.S. government seeking one hundred thousand dollars as compensation for his arrest, wrongful imprisonment, and loss of his health due to lead poisoning from the prison paint shop. Harrison represented all the army officers and soldiers that were involved in the military trial.

Consistent with memories that stressed the importance of reflecting on one's duties and taking responsibility for one's own actions, Harrison developed a convincing argument that the military personnel had acted with a sense of duty and responsibility. He argued that even if Milligan was justified in asking for damages the individual sacrifices made by the soldiers and their families justified their actions and mitigated the need for a large settlement. In his oral argument he stated:

> *I pity the man that can listen to such stories of wrong, conspiracy, and treason, and not find his heart all aglow with honest indignation ... They were United States soldiers who heard the cry of national distress, and with brave, true hearts, had forsaken all and dared all, that they might preserve us as a nation.*

According to biographer Harry Sievers, "As a piece of oratory and special pleading, Harrison's summation was masterful." The memories served as helpful sidebars, reminding Harrison that devotion to duty and responsibility mattered in a case where a "traitor"—now freed—could be unfairly compensated. The memories influenced the way he thought about this case and of his own role as a lawyer. The court ruled that the government owed Milligan compensation—but only the sum of five dollars. The victory enhanced Harrison's reputation as a masterful defense attorney and furthered his political ambitions.

In 1876 Harrison was selected by the Republican state committee to run for governor three months before the election, after the Republican candidate was accused of financial wrongdoing, and had to withdraw from the race. Harrison lost the race; and one factor that contributed to the loss was the lack of time to campaign. He was also defeated by the stand-offish manner that the memories foreshadowed. For example, he was described as "cold-blooded as a fish" and "a stinking little aristocrat who never recognized men on the street." Once, when a politician was asked if he would board "the Harrison bandwagon," he replied, "I never ride an ice-cart." Another politician remarked that he could be "as glacial as a Siberian stripped of his furs."

The unflattering comments offered a picture of Harrison's behavior that was dramatically at odds with his preferred view of himself in the first memory—that is, a religious person who, like his mother, kept his distance in order to better reflect on his commitment to social justice, family, country and the Presbyterian faith. The image of someone who had built an ice-wall around himself thoroughly captured the downside of his introverted temperament.

The clash between his self-identity and how others saw him created a form of cognitive dissonance, and sometimes that dissonance caused him to further disengage. In this light, in a manner consistent with his dour temperament, he once said about himself, "I am born to be a drudge." Even if Harrison "remembered the awe he felt at the nightly ritual of his mother withdrawing from the family circle to commune alone" he may have felt trapped in his own inner circle, where the outside was hard to reach and the way out seemed risky. As Harrison commented, "I always carry care and responsibility heavily." Perhaps when others characterized him as remote or stand-offish he would find solace in prayer. As he wrote to his son, "Prayer steadies one when he is walking in slippery places, even if things asked for are not given."

Senator and President

By 1880 the Civil War hero had achieved national prominence as a politician. President James Garfield offered Harrison a cabinet post, which he declined in order to strengthen his political standing within his own state. In 1881 the Indiana state legislature elected him to the U. S. Senate. As a senator Harrison supported mainstream Republican legislation including pensions for Civil War veterans; admission of several new western states; strengthening the Navy; and imposing high tariffs to protect American workers. Departing from the Republican party line, he declined to support the Chinese Exclusion Act which was designed to prohibit Chinese immigration into the U. S. for twenty years, and prevent Chinese people living here from becoming citizens. During his term he promoted conservation, and recommended setting aside land that would eventually lead to the creation of the Grand Canyon National Park.

In 1887 Harrison lost his bid for reelection to the Senate because Democrats had taken over the Indiana legislature and they appointed a Democrat to replace him. As a result, he returned to Indiana and began to lay the foundation for his candidacy in the next presidential election. In 1888, after the eighth ballot, he was nominated at the Republican convention as a compromise candidate.

Harrison conducted the nation's first "front porch" campaign. From the front steps of his home, he gave nearly one hundred speeches to as many as three hundred thousand people. Conversely, President Cleveland did not campaign during the election believing that the President should be above partisan campaigning. Speaking to large crowds several times a day, Harrison overextended himself, which led to a mix of physical and emotional exhaustion. The fear of straying from his path of duty, as suggested in the memory, contributed to his exhaustion. A newspaperman close to the campaign remarked, "He had grown cross and ill-tempered even to those of his family … but if he can control his nervous exhaustion, he may get through the campaign all right."

During the campaign Harrison's public interactions were influenced more by the first memory, in which being closed-off was a virtue rather than a liability. This was evident in a series of speeches he made during a railroad campaign through Indiana. A political friend of his, John Wise, described what happened at one train stop:

> *The crowds who listened to him would become wildly enthusiastic. Then he would hold the reception in the car and the people, after shaking hands with him, would pass out of the other end of the car silent and depressed, as if suffering from a chill. A wag in the party pulled the bell-rope and started the train as soon as Harrison stopped speaking. When chided for it he said: "Don't talk to me. I know my business. Ben Harrison had the crowd red-hot. I did not want him to freeze it out of them with his handshaking."*

In the presidential election, Cleveland won the popular vote but Harrison won in the Electoral College. By winning the election he achieved an important milestone; that is, he proved himself worthy and fulfilled the expectations of his family legacy. Now he could publicly recognize the importance of his connection to his grandfather, rather than distancing himself from him as he did in the second memory, when he asserted, "I am the grandson of nobody." In turn, his campaign supporters passed out handbills and souvenirs picturing him and his grandfather together, reminding Americans of the connection between the two famous Generals and Presidents.

After the election, Senator Matthew Quay of Pennsylvania, who was also chairman of the Republican National Committee, went to Indianapolis to congratulate Harrison. In the end, the narrow victory depended on close margins in key states such as Pennsylvania, where the Quay machine produced a dubious margin of victory by falsifying voting records. In return, Quay expected political favors such as patronage positions. He was surprised when Harrison said, "Providence has given us the victory." Quay responded, "He ought to know that Providence hadn't a damn thing to do with it ... he would never know how close a number of men were compelled to approach the penitentiary to make him President."

Harrison's response to Quay was consistent with his sense of himself in the first memory as a religious person but it was inconsistent with Quay's expectation for a *quid pro quo*. In the past, and now as President, he felt beholden to no one except himself and God.

During his presidency Harrison was committed to the beliefs and values that were contained in the memory. For instance, in his Inaugural Address he called upon God to bestow on him "wisdom, strength, and fidelity." A description of him in the New York Tribune revealed his preference for solitary reflection: "He was of a deliberate habit of mind and not only took his own time but kept his own counsel." Moreover, as President, fundamental questions posed by his religious faith guided his thought process—questions such as what political, social and economic policies have value and are worth striving for? What values transcend political expediency? During his presidency, Harrison applied these ethical questions to a variety of issues such as social justice and civil rights for African-Americans. His commitment to social justice inspired him to appoint the civil rights leader, Frederick Douglass, as U. S. ambassador to Haiti.

In addition, to protect the voting rights of African-Americans he supported legislation for a Voting Rights Act that allowed the federal government to supervise voter registration and elections in the south. This legislation was ahead of its time and failed to pass, and it was not until 1965 that Congress passed a federal law protecting minority citizens' voting rights. While the civil rights challenges people faced in the 1960's were different from those Harrison encountered, the values of social justice and civil rights that guided Presidents Lyndon Johnson and Benjamin Harrison were the same.

During his presidency, Carrie Harrison was an active First Lady. She installed the first Christmas tree in the White House and became the first president of the Daughters of the American Revolution. Under her leadership, she began the White House china collection and for the first time electric lights were installed at the White House—even though she was too frightened of the switches to turn them on! Carrie and her husband continued the practice of daily prayer that was highlighted in the first memory. As one observer wrote, "No morning is passed in the White House and no day's duties or pleasures are begun without the brief family prayer."

The solitude foreshadowed in the memory significantly influenced Harrison's leadership style. He felt he had a responsibility to set himself apart and be his own person. He spent long periods of time in solitary contemplation rather than engaging with others. As he put it, "There is a great sense of loneliness in the discharge of high public duties. The moment of decision is one of isolation."

But there was a price to be paid for his isolation—it contributed to the perception that he was unapproachable. While his principles may have been thoughtful his actions could be self-defeating, alienating people who might otherwise have supported him. For example, a Civil War veteran who had lost an arm solicited a patronage appointment. As he made his case, Harrison interrupted him by saying, "Oh, I know all about the political conditions up there much better than you." The veteran responded, "Do you mean to tell me that you know more about the political conditions in my home district where I have lived all my life than I do?" Harrison replied, "Certainly, you have only the narrow personal interest view and do not comprehend the real situation." The veteran responded, "Then I have nothing more to say, good day, Mr. President."

A friend commented that Harrison was "the only man I ever saw who could do another man a favor in such a way that all the sweetness and appreciation and sense of gratitude was gone from it, and this was the trouble with him in many instances." Harrison was chided for requiring office-seekers to present their case for patronage while standing in front of him as he anxiously drummed his fingers on the desk. One politician said talking to Harrison was like "talking to a hitching post," and Matthew Quay described him as "all ears and no tongue." A governor calling at the White House with business to transact was offended by his gruff greeting: "I've got all these papers to look after, and I am going fishing at 2 o'clock." In this long series of plodding social missteps, he crossed a line between being characteristically blunt and insultingly dismissive.

Harrison understood leadership in a way often lost on more socially conscious Presidents who prioritized being "likeable" and "approachable" as essential attributes for effective governance. Harrison was brusque and seemed incapable of being familiar, especially with strangers. Instead, he was faithful to the memory in which his revered mother was portrayed as a singular figure who aspired to achieve inner peace by setting herself apart. He could be apprehensive about delegating advanced responsibility to others that he considered of lesser talent—but that style of leadership did have its advantages. One senator offered his opinion that,

> *Harrison was the only man who had ever been president who was capable of discharging with single ability the duty of every one of his cabinet ministers; that he was the best equipped man that had ever been in public life.*

In the area of foreign affairs Harrison supported the expansion of the U. S. Navy into a world-class fleet of seven armored ships, setting the stage for the U. S. to eventually become a world power. He sought to expand U. S. power in Latin America by increasing trade agreements with them. This led seventeen countries to convene with U. S. officials at the Pan-American conference, the first such trade meeting with Latin America. He negotiated the establishment of a protectorate over the Samoan Islands with Germany and Great Britain, and successfully opposed the destruction of the seal population by hunters in the Bering Sea. Harrison threatened to use the force of the Navy to keep Great Britain and Canada from hunting the seals in waters next to Alaska. His active and dynamic agenda was credited as being a model for Teddy Roosevelt and William McKinley, both of whom later emulated Harrison's tenacity and bold leadership in the area of foreign affairs.

In the area of domestic affairs, six new states joined the Union, the most admitted during any presidential administration. Harrison also supported the McKinley Tariff Act which significantly raised tariffs on imported goods; the Sherman Antitrust Act which restricted trusts and gave the federal government the power to regulate and sue big businesses; the Forest Reserve Act which permitted the government to create national forest and wilderness preserves; and the Sherman Silver Purchase Act which permitted the Treasury Department to accept silver as well as gold to back up paper money. And for the first time, Congress approved legislation that provided pensions for Civil War veterans, and for their widows and children. The Republican majority in Congress passed so much costly legislation that they were referred to as "the Billion-Dollar Congress," to which one politician retorted, "Yes, but it's a billion-dollar country!"

In contrast to his reputation as an advocate for African-Americans, Harrison's reputation for dealing with Native-Americans was compromised. For instance, he sent thousands of soldiers to South Dakota's Wounded Knee Creek, where the Lakota Sioux were trying to hold onto their land. A battle occurred as soldiers attempted to disarm some of the Native-Americans, leaving twenty-five soldiers dead along with more than one hundred Native-Americans, including many women and children. The massacre at Wounded Knee was the last major clash between U. S. soldiers and Native-Americans. Harrison lamented the overall treatment of Native-Americans, but as President he believed that his first duty was to preserve the political and social order of the Union.

Harrison was a supporter of civil service reform and offered Theodore Roosevelt the post of Civil Service Commissioner. Roosevelt later remarked that Harrison "gave me my first opportunity to do big things." In 1892, workers went on strike in Pennsylvania at a steel plant owned by Andrew Carnegie. The strike led to violent confrontations between police and the strikers, and in one case a gun battle killed twenty men. Late in his term, Harrison attempted to annex the Hawaiian Islands. Although the U. S. ambassador to Hawaii claimed that it was now part of the United States, Congress refused to act on the annexation before the end of his term, leaving it to the next president to make the decision.

Harrison was uncertain about running for a second term. He had accumulated many enemies, such as Quay, who felt they had not been properly rewarded with patronage jobs. Even members from his own party found it difficult to endorse him given his prickly disposition. Others were alienated by his support for controversial policies, such as imposing tariffs that brought large profits to big business but failed to raise wages or improve working conditions. Moreover, violent strikes turned labor against him believing that he was siding with big business instead of workers. One final factor that led to his unpopularity was the publication of Jacob Riis's *How the Other Half Lives*. This book documented deplorable living conditions such as overcrowding and inadequate sanitation, especially in urban tenements. Nevertheless, only a few weeks before the convention Harrison decided to run, declaring, "No Harrison has ever retreated in the presence of a foe without giving battle, and so I have determined to stand and fight."

Unlike his first presidential election, Harrison did not actively campaign. He removed himself from the campaign trail to be at his wife's side, who was dying of tuberculosis. In the first memory, Harrison's mother demonstrated her lasting commitment to family above all else. Similarly, during the election, Harrison committed himself to supporting his wife and family above all else, even at the cost of losing a second term. Carrie Harrison died in the White House in 1892.

Harrison soundly lost the election, and even lost in his home state of Indiana. He confided to a friend, "Indeed after the heavy blow the death of my wife dealt me, I do not think I could have stood the strain a reelection would have brought," and he told his family that he felt he had been "freed from prison."

In a way Harrison's introverted personality was a self-imposed prison. He was ambitious and aspired to live up to the expectations of his family name; but sentencing himself to solitary confinement made it difficult to project qualities such as warmth and empathy that were necessary to relate well to others and gain acceptance.

Elder Statesman

Harrison pursued charitable work after his presidency. Under the auspices of the Presbyterian Church in which he held a national office, he donated money to further education for African-Americans in the south. He served on the advisory board of the Indianapolis Orphan Asylum; served as a trustee of Purdue University; taught a class on constitutional law at Stanford University; and attended the First Peace Conference at The Hague. In 1896, to the surprise of his family, Harrison married Mary Lord Dimmick, his deceased wife's niece and nearly 30 years his junior. His children were upset about it and refused to attend the wedding. Using themes contained in the memory, he explained his decision to his son: "I am sure my children will not wish me to live the years that remain to me in solitude."

In 1897 Harrison and his second wife had a daughter, Elizabeth, whom they named after Harrison's mother. He appeared to enjoy his new "family circle" and tried to spend as much time as possible at home in order to be with his family. In 1899 he served as chief counsel for Venezuela in a territorial dispute with British Guiana. Once again, his tendency to overwork became a problem. He told a colleague, "I have been working every day this summer except Sundays, and I find myself almost to the breaking point."

In making the legal case for Venezuela before the international tribunal in Paris, Harrison characteristically relied on facts and logic rather than charisma. For example, in a manner consistent with his legalistic and formal style he submitted to the court an eight-hundred page "brief" whereas Great Britain's submission was sixty-five pages. Even beyond that, he presented twenty-five hours of oral argument over the course of five days. Harrison lost the case, but his thoughtful, detailed and cerebral arguments enhanced his reputation as an expert international lawyer.

In 1901 Harrison died of pneumonia. Thousands of soldiers and survivors of his Civil War regiment attended the funeral. Historian Henry Adams wrote, "He was an excellent President, a man of ability and force; perhaps the best President the Republican Party had put forward since Lincoln's death." Poet James Whitcomb Riley celebrated him at the funeral for his "fearless independence and stand for what he believed to be right and just."

Summary

In Memory One Harrison modeled himself after the example set by his mother—that it is important to withdraw into prayer for things other than our own security and advancement. The long shadow of the memory can be seen in his belief that in being his own person he could enhance his self-worth and carry the legacy of his family forward. Of course, when he set himself apart and played emotional solitaire he encountered problems, such as his disregard for the sensitivities of others, appearing distant as if he were an intellectual hermit, or possessed an air of superior intelligence.

The ultimate meaning of the first memory is not so easily determined. Does it represent his impulse to detach himself from others? Or does it reveal his preference for solitary thinking over teamwork? Does it mark the beginning of the idea that he was as answerable to himself as much as to the world? Elements of these ideas and others reflect the complexity of the memory and help to explain its honored place among his childhood recollections—and continued to reverberate far beyond the confines of the family circle in which it took place.

In Memory Two we see that Harrison was a complex figure, concerned about demonstrating an independent image yet dependent on a need to prove himself to others. Throughout his life, the determination to keep the "Harrison legacy" alive was as burdensome as it was sustaining. His methodical, "follow-the-facts" thinking style co-existed with a reserved and stoic manner that was often perceived as aloof or stand-offish. In the end, his "first-class intellect," ambitiousness and family name certainly helped; but so did his memories because they inspired him to set aside a contemplative space where he could be an original rather than a copy of the other members of his renowned family.

The following is an excerpt from a statement Harrison once commented about Abraham Lincoln:

> *The course before him was lighted only by the lamp of duty; outside its radiance all was dark. He seemed to me to be conscious of all this, to be weighted by it, but so strong was his sense of duty, so courageous his heart, so sure was he of his own high purposes and motives and of the favor of God for himself and his people, that he moved forward calmly to his appointed work; not with show or brag, neither with shrinking.*

This statement reflected the essential message of both memories and Harrison's self-perception. He viewed himself as dutiful and courageous of heart; but so conflicted about his "own high purposes and motives" that he would "shrink"—distance himself—from others so they would not feel insecure or threatened by his presence or his illustrious family name.

The two compelling memories suggested that Harrison was appreciative of his "dark" side—his solitude—which provided comfort and strength from the power of prayer; and the "light" side which radiated from his elevated heritage. Solitude allowed Harrison to locate the "sacred space" inside of himself where he could reflect on his own thoughts and feelings; whereas presenting himself as independent of the family name provided the moral resolve and strength required to act.

Bibliography

Calhoun, Charles. Benjamin Harrison. The American Presidents
Series: New York Times Books, 2005.
   A brief but incisive analysis of Harrison's life and political legacy.

Harrison, Benjamin. Views of an Ex-President. Compiled by Mary
Lord Harrison. Indianapolis, Bowen-Merrill, 1901.

Richardson, James D. A Compilation of the Messages and Papers of
the Presidents. Volume 9, part one: Benjamin Harrison. A Public
Domain Book, Published by Congress, 1902.

Socolofsky, Homer E., and Allan B. Spetter. The presidency of
Benjamin Harrison. Lawrence: University Press of Kansas,1987.

Sievers, Harry J. Benjamin Harrison: Hoosier Warrior, 1833–1865.
University Publishers Inc. New York, 1952.
   *The most comprehensive account of Harrison's early life that
   covers his birth through his military service in the Civil War.
   The detailed footnotes are insightful and the writing style is
   compelling.*

Sievers, Harry J. Benjamin Harrison: Hoosier Statesman, 1865-1888.
University Publishers Inc. New York, 1959.

Sievers, Harry J. Benjamin Harrison: Hoosier President, 1889-1901.
The Bobbs–Merrill Company, Inc. Indianapolis, 1968.

Wallace, Lew. Life of Gen. Ben Harrison. Philadelphia: Hubbard
Brothers, 1888.

Wise, John S. Recollections of Thirteen Presidents. Freeport, New
York: Books for Libraries Press, 1968.

Conclusion

This book has attempted to examine the personality of eight Presidents from the perspective of their most compelling early memories. It views their character from a symbolic angle that is replete with dramatic characters, fortunes made and reversals of fortune, optimism and pessimism. While an early memory cannot predict events or supply definitive answers about a person's character or actions, it can provide an interpretive framework in which self-identity emerges. In this light, an early memory is, in a sense, "whispering your intentions to yourself" before they are "shouted to the world" in the form of action.

The different layers of an early memory—how the teller perceives the past, present and future—can be compared to the different layers (branches) of government: legislative, executive and judicial. Just as the divisions of the United States government help prevent abuses of power, since each branch has to answer to the other two, so too memories contain three layers or branches that help the teller to look at his life from multiple angles.

The checks and balances that define our constitutional system of government rely on all three branches working together in the spirit of cooperation. Similarly, to examine an early memory effectively it is important to interpret the narrative through the interplay of all three dimensions: past, present and future. In doing so, one is more likely to generate a meaningful interpretation. When Benjamin Franklin was asked, "What have we got—a republic or a monarchy?" He responded, "A republic, if you can keep it." It might be said of an early memory that it is "an enlightenment, if you can examine it."

About the Author

Henry J. Roth, Ph.D., received his doctorate in Special Education, School Psychology and Counseling Psychology from Duke University in Durham, North Carolina. He has been the Principal of therapeutic day schools in Durham and Chicago; and Executive Director of the Sonia Shankman Orthogenic School at the University of Chicago. He has been an adjunct instructor in Special Education at Northeastern Illinois University, and most recently at George Mason and Trinity Washington universities.

Over his career, Henry has employed early memories as an effective diagnostic and therapeutic counseling technique. In occasionally running across a president's memory in his reading, Henry became interested in finding other presidents' memories and analyzing how they helped to shape their character and actions. This book grew out of that interest.

If you have any comments or questions that you would like to ask Henry, he can be reached at:

HenryRoth2003@gmail.com